Christian Growth
B O O K S

Dealing
with Your
Discontent

HOW TO OVERCOME
DISSATISFACTION

Peter L. Steinke

AUGSBURG Publishing House • Minneapolis

To Bertha Rode
my grandmother whose life
has been woven through both
contentment and discontent
yet lives with vigor and joy
in this the year of
her 100th birthday.

DEALING WITH YOUR DISCONTENT
How to Overcome Dissatisfaction

Copyright © 1988 Augsburg Publishing House

Scripture quotations unless otherwise noted are from the Holy Bible: New International Version. Copyright 1978 by the New York International Bible Society. Use by permission of Zondervan Bible Publishers.

Scripture quotations marked TEV are from The Good News Bible, Today's English Version, copyright 1966, 1971, 1976 by American Bible Society. Used by permission.

Library of Congress Cataloging-in-Publication Data

Steinke, Peter L.
 DEALING WITH YOUR DISCONTENT.

 (Christian growth books)
 1. Christian life—1960–   2. Discontent.
I. Title. II. Series.
BV4501.2.S7539   1988   248.8'6   88-6265
ISBN 0-8066-2307-1

Manufactured in the U.S.A.   APH 10-1842

1   2   3   4   5   6   7   8   9   0   1   2   3   4   5   6   7   8   9

Contents

Editor's Foreword

Christian life—like all life—is dynamic. It has direction and involves growth. "Instead, by speaking the truth in a spirit of love, we must grow up in every way to Christ, who is the head" (Eph. 4:15 TEV). God *calls* us to grow. "Grow in the grace and knowledge of our Lord and Savior Jesus Christ" (2 Peter 3:18). We grow in what God has given us—the grace of being in a relationship with him.

Christian growth is both personal and corporate. Living in interdependence with others, we grow within the Christian community—the body of Christ. This growth is the work of the Holy Spirit. Paul spelled it out clearly: "The fruit of the Spirit is love, joy, peace, patience, kindness, goodness, faithfulness, gentleness and self-control" (Gal. 5:22).

Although the analogy is from nature's growth from blossom to fruit, Christian growth is not completed in our lifetime. We are always moving, but never arriving. Actually we grow in our *awareness* of our need for growth. And Christian growth may not be as observable to the senses as is nature's fruit. It is patterned after the crucifixion and resurrection of Christ. The experience is seldom steady and gradual. The way *up* may be the way *down*. The new comes out of the death of the old.

Christian growth is therefore a venture of faith that focuses on forgiveness. It happens in response to God's call and is secured only by God's grace.

God calls us to grow by creating within us a desire for it. "As a deer longs for a stream of cool water, so I long for you, O God" (Ps. 42:1 TEV). Peter also described this desire: "Crave pure spiritual milk, so that by it you may grow up in your salvation, now that you have tasted that the Lord is good" (1 Peter 2:2). Jesus described it as "hungering and thirsting." "Blessed are those who hunger and thirst for righteousness, for they will be filled" (Matt. 5:6).

The books in this series are intended as helps in this pilgrimage of growth. Each one deals with a particular facet of this adventure. Growth takes place in interaction with the human community. It involves not only our relationship with God but also our relationship with people. Peter Steinke is both a theologian and a psychologist. He effectively combines these disciplines in this book to help us receive the spiritual quality of contentment. The emphasis is on *receiving* because Steinke clearly shows how we contribute to our discontent through protective illusions, wishful thinking, and a victim mentality.

Through a careful analysis of our unrealistic beliefs and expectations, the author leads us to a perspective on life that is in harmony with a fallen world and with the gospel of hope. With his creative questionnaires he helps us to assess where we are at present in our life, and on the basis of this assessment, to develop a self-image that is neither too negative nor too positive.

Steinke utilizes the Bible to envision a contentment that is consonant with our Christian growth. Of equal importance, he describes the steps that we can take to receive this contentment.

WILLIAM E. HULME

Preface

Discontent is your restless desire for something more or different, something pleasing or purposeful. One writer compares discontent to a person crawling across the desert. He wants only water, but once he gets his drink, he wants theater tickets. Discontent, driven by desire, is your argument with life.

This book is about discontent, and, too, it is about contentment. The word *content* literally means "keep together." You are content when you feel whole, not torn apart by restless desire. In the British House of Lords, *content* signifies an affirmative vote, similar to the expression, "aye." Contentment is saying "yes" to life.

We know some things about the problem of discontent, yet we do not know how discontent can be resolved for any single person. Likewise, "the overriding fact is that no one factor or small set of factors *determines* happiness," states Jonathan Freedman, author of *Happy People* (New York: Ballantine Books, 1978). "People find happiness in all sorts of ways, in all sorts of situations." The one thing we know, though, is that both discontent and contentment are always *personal*. We participate in our own dissatisfaction as well as in our own satisfaction. Discontent and contentment are decisions we make.

Contentment is, for instance, not something you touch, like a leaf, or see, like a sunset. Contentment is *in* yourself. It does not arise because of your fate, your stars, or your circumstances. You are as contented as you choose to be. Truer yet, contentment is what you choose to be again and again and again. It is one of those realities only you can teach yourself. You are responsible for your contentment in the world you make.

In constructing a world of contentment, we do not have the same materials with which to build. But we participate in the same project—building a life of satisfaction and purpose with whatever materials we have. I invite you to explore with me how we design our worlds by the choices we make. You will not discover a 10-step promise to 100% satisfaction; you will not find a secret formula for putting paradise in your pocket. What you will encounter is my vision of a life you can enjoy when you choose to enjoy it.

This book is divided into three parts. In Part 1, "The Way You See Things," you are introduced to how your inner world affects the way you live. Chapter 1, "The World inside You," describes how you form mental pictures from your experiences, and how those images affect whether you view life as painful or pleasurable. Your "pictured" world is maintained by your beliefs, wishes, and expectations. These have positive effects in your life, yet they contain the germs of discontent. Beliefs are discussed in Chapter 2, "Setting Yourself Up for Disappointment"; wishes are confronted in Chapter 3, "Loosening the Grip of Wishful Thinking"; expectations are the core of "Finding the Missing X" in Chapter 4.

Part 2, "How You Deal with Your Discontent," looks at three overreactive ways of coming to terms with your discontent. "Taking a Psychological Bath," Chapter 5, looks at blaming. Brooding and banishing are discussed in Chapter 6, "Who Said Life Was Fair?" A realistic and hopeful method—taking responsibility for who you are and the world you create—is the topic of Chapter 7, "Contentment Is Yours."

Part 3, "Making Changes in Your Life," draws your attention to visions of growth. "When Discontent Is a Blessing," Chapter 8, focuses on contentment arising from struggle because contentment is found within real-life problems. Discontent can be turned into a force for change, a motivation for the search for a richer life. "The Restless Heart," Chapter 9, covers spiritual themes and resources for dealing with discontent and recognizing faith as a way of experiencing the world. Chapter 10, "Stepping into the Picture," illustrates how psychological and spiritual growth helps you live creatively with your restless need for fulfillment.

An appendix with activities for each of the 10 chapters is added. They can be completed individually for self-reflection or used in a study group for discussion.

Part One

The Way
You See Things

1

The World inside You

You create a world out of your experiences. Your experiences become pictures in your mind. They make your world familiar. Feelings—either painful or pleasurable—are associated with the pictures. You act to reduce the pain and to increase the pleasure. When you experience pain, you are discontented. If you picture yourself living under the control of your discontent, you feel helpless and hopeless, as if you have no other choice. You *condition* yourself to act in this way. But you can imagine another picture and make a new choice.

Overwhelmed

You deal with an endless parade of disappointments every day—from a flat tire on the freeway to an inflamed tooth on Friday; from forgetting your house key to remembering your stained dress; from the loss of a job promotion to the gain of a stress-induced headache; from yesterday's blunder to this morning's argument with your spouse. Disappointments are part of living—and they are the seeds of discontent.

Once disappointment swells, you may react by verbally attacking someone or brooding in a swamp of self-pity. You may become numb. If your swollen frustration persists, you become exhausted—near the point of hopelessness.

The feeling of disappointment itself never signals danger, not even the angering, depressing, or numbing that may follow. These are human reactions in the service of survival. The danger always lies in being *overwhelmed* by your experience. You allow yourself to become captive to your feelings of discouragement. Listen to your description of yourself as "feeling low" and "let down." These feelings immobilize you. You begin to think and act like a victim. Again, listen to your description of your experience as "the bottom's falling out" and "things are going to pieces." You live as if there are no other choices or responses available to you. Although you feel overpowered, actually you give your power away. Conversely, you do not experience your own power to respond in a new or different way. You are stuck in your appraisal of what is happening around and within you. The only resolution, you think, is despair.

The downward steps of discontent are portrayed below:

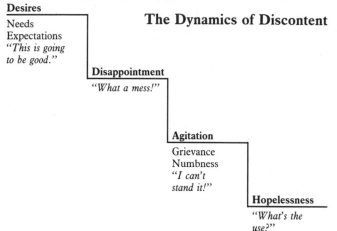

Desires

Needs
Expectations
*"This is going
to be good."*

The Dynamics of Discontent

Disappointment

"What a mess!"

Agitation

Grievance
Numbness
*"I can't
stand it!"*

Hopelessness

*"What's the
use?"*

No one is complete. Your desires, needs, and expectations point to your limits and dependencies. Besides your incompleteness, you come up against life's limitations. Disappointment, the first stage of discontent, is the experience of something missing, something imperfect. To protect yourself and guard against hurt, you react. But if the intensity and duration of both the hurt and the reaction overtake you, you grow weary of it all.

How you see things

Flat tires. Headaches. Arguments. Every day hundreds of things happen to you. Sometimes you react in anger or fear; sometimes you respond by asserting yourself and making choices. Either is the outcome of the way you perceive things. Your perceptions shape and color your world. What you "see" is what you get. Contentment, like beauty, is in the eyes of the beholder. As for discontent, John Powell notes in *The Christian Vision:* "The monkeys on our backs are really born in our minds." What matters most is your appraisal of what is happening, how you see reality, the way you take it. "Man is troubled not by things," an ancient philosopher said, "but by the view he takes of them."

Neurologist Paul MacLean sets forth a model of the human brain with three levels (described in Charles Hampden-Turner, *Maps of the Mind* [New York: Collier Books, 1982]). Each level has its own function. His model illustrates how your perception constructs your world.

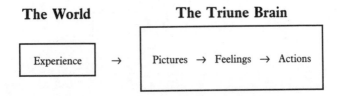

The World	The Triune Brain
Experience →	Pictures → Feelings → Actions

Learning begins with experience. Your experiences are imprinted in the brain as pictures. This largest part of your brain is like a shed in which tools, materials, and pieces of equipment are stored. Over a period of years, it becomes a storehouse of many resources. Similarly, the brain is a storage shed of thousands of images. The pictures most deeply embedded in your brain are those formed in emotionally-charged experiences. Some of your pictures evoke pleasant feelings, others unpleasant ones. In turn, these feelings activate certain types of behavior, such as fighting, fleeing, or clutching.

MacLean's model is illustrated from my own experience. Around the age of five, I climbed a tree to escape a neighbor's German Shepherd dog whose barking terrified me. In my mental shed, there is a picture of this dog. Today when I see a German Shepherd dog, my emotion is fear. I freeze motionless just as I did on the tree limb years ago.

Consider the experiences of people discussed in two articles written by *Chicago Tribune* columnist Bob Greene. In the first article ("Pain That Won't Go Away," *The Dallas Morning News,* Dec. 18, 1985) Greene disclosed a trick played on a 12-year-old seventh grader. Classmates put a card, headlined "Most Unpopular Student Award," on the boy's desk and filled in his name. The boy was devastated. After this article appeared, Greene wrote a follow-up editorial, surprised at the number of respondents to the first article. Readers recounted their own experiences of unpopularity in their youth. Old pictures stirred once again, even in the minds of adults who were successful. "I'm surprised I had the strength to make it through that period of my life," one reader stated, "Now I have a family and a good job and a lot of friends. But whenever I'm feeling down, I realize that inside of me that little boy still lives; the little boy who sat alone at home because nobody wanted to play with him." Others reported feelings of shame and thoughts of being at fault for not being liked. "There's no one to blame," one reader recalls, "so you end up blaming yourself." Humiliating experiences caused persons to see themselves as unpopular and these pictures became imprinted in the brain. Many changed their inner pictures, but none forgot. Greene's article triggered the old image in their mental shed.

What happens in you

Something traumatic happens to you. The happening can be neither modified nor changed, maybe not even explained. The experience is stored in the brain and remembered as painful. Later events similar to the original one can arouse the picture.

Early life events influence and inform your world. As they occur you design an inner world full of pictures. As an infant you lived in a world where you were acted upon, where what you needed rested outside of yourself. You reacted. As you developed, you stored your emotion-charged images in your head. You started to live *within*. You built an inner world (pictures/feelings) out of the outer world (experiences), then you lived in the inner world to deal with the outer world.

When you are anxious you often fall back, not surprisingly, to feelings of helplessness, or you turn to childish behavior to defend yourself or get what you need. That's the way you learned to handle life when you were young. So now you may let others tell you what to do rather than choose for yourself. You look outside yourself, at the events, instead of examining the picture/feelings of your inner world. Many stubbornly believe that misery happens to them, that others make them unhappy, that the world causes their troubles, that unexpected events control them. Like infants, they live as if they are helpless, as if what they need is only outside of themselves.

A husband complained to me about his wife's cold silence. As far as he was concerned, she represented an icy, distant woman. His perception of her changed, however, when he discovered in counseling that his mother had used sullen stares to punish him. His wife's silence triggered an old, hurtful image.

With another couple, a wife came to realize that her husband's angry voice activated an old ache, a picture of her father who had shouted at her abusively when she was a child. Whenever her husband raised his voice, the image in her head clicked on with the message, "there's nothing there for me but agony."

In both instances the spouses initially perceived the problem to be outside of themselves, when in reality, the difficulty involved their interaction with their partners. The husband's loud voice, for instance, triggered the wife's painful picture from her past. She was reacting to something within herself. When she became *aware* of what was happening, she informed her husband of her negative picture of a ranting male. Moreover, she accepted her own appraisal—loudness equals abuse—as her contribution to their marital trouble. Instead of blaming her husband, she asked him to change the tone of his voice when he spoke to her. She changed her energies from self-defense (reaction) to creative effort (response).

Discontent and contentment depend, not on what simply happens *to* you, but on what is significantly happening *in* you. The movement from disappointment and despair to hope is a matter of reappraisal, of seeing things with new images.

What's your explanation

The studies of Martin Seligman ("Stop Blaming Yourself," *Psychology Today*, Feb. 1987, pp. 31-39) add another dimension to perceptual appraisal. He discovered that the *way* you explain what happens to you influences *how* you deal with your life. You not only have emotionally-impacted mental pictures in your brain but also *explanatory styles*, ways you interpret your experience. He cites three styles which distort your thinking in a negative way:

Stable style—"I always mess up."

"It'll last forever."

Global style—"I can't do anything right."

"It's going to ruin everything I do."

Internal style—"All my fault . . ."

"There's nothing good about me."

If you use these pessimistic explanations, you leave yourself in a defensive position. Rather than being responsive, you are reactive. "What can I do?" Obviously, nothing. You give up your power and lose the sense of being responsible for yourself (stable, global). Or you turn the sword inward, on yourself (internal). With explanations such as these, there is nothing worth attaining, nothing worth risking.

But the three styles serve a purpose. They maintain the images in your mental shed. I discover many people whose explanatory style indicates self-disdain. They always *evaluate* their experiences negatively instead of *describing* them factually. Some may have never outgrown the childish thought that the world owes them something, hence they use one or all of the styles to maneuver someone to take care of them. Others choose to remain with their *known* misery rather than risk *unknown* experiences. And a number of them, overwhelmed by negative life experiences, are fearful of being hurt again. They will use pessimistic explanations to avoid feeling the original pain. While explanatory styles defend their fragile selves, they do not develop their creative imagination—*new* pictures of themselves.

The picture processing

You experience life and register it in your brain, where it becomes imprinted and is associated with either pain or pleasure. This can be triggered again by the course of events.

Two years ago on Christmas Eve my car would not start. Only a few days before I paid a repair bill of $500. My picture of a reliable car, especially after a $500 charge, did not fit with the car's failure to operate. I was caught between my picture of the mechanic's competency, fairness, and past reliability and a car that would not start. Discontented, to say the least, I wondered why I purchased this "lemon" and why I selected this "sorry" mechanic. I even feared that the mechanic was "out to get me." I reacted.

Now my car's problem *activated* these feelings and thoughts. But my car's problem did not *cause* my reactions. I was the *cause* of my *effects*. I *choose* them; I *generated* them. After all, I could have chosen to laugh about what happened or try to find out why. What happened happened. I could do nothing to change the circumstance, but I could have changed my inner pictures and feelings.

There is no doubt that you and I live reflexively, without prior thought. We live with *conditioned responses*. We put our lives on "cruise control." Consequently we act without intention or awareness. But we do not *only* live this way. We are capable of *creative imagination*. Conditioned responses are based on *cause* and *effect*. If you, for example, complain to your wife, "You make me angry," there is a situation of cause (you) and effect (angry). But if you would say to her, "I am angry, but I don't want to get into a fight," you are making a choice. *You are processing a picture.* The two charts below distinguish the difference between conditioned response and creative imagination.

Conditioned response

Cause	*Effect*
My car will not start, even after paying a repair bill of $500.	I am angry with the car, the mechanic, and myself. I have the "paranoid" thought that the repair shop is deceiving me.

When I accept "conditioned response," I believe my car's problems cause my thoughts and feelings. I am conditioned to react in this way; "I'm only human. What else could I do?" In reality, though, this is the "I'm-only-an-animal" explanation of behavior. For we share with animals the last level of MacLean's scheme of the brain, the smallest part where action originates. With some animals we share the middle level, that of feeling. But we do not share with animals the first level—the large, elaborate portion of the brain where thinking occurs and pictures are interpreted. Thus we are not automatically conditioned to react in determined ways. We do not enter the door of cause and pass through to the next door of effect. We can create new pictures. We have the capacity to influence what we feel and do because of our human brain, our unique perspective. True, we cannot control everything. That's the illusion of omnipotence. Nevertheless, alongside of our limits and conditioning, there is the ability to make new or different appraisals. As Viktor Frankl says in *Man's Search for Meaning*, the last human freedom available is one's attitude toward life. The next chart illustrates that possibility.

Creative imagination

Event	Inner picture	Cause	Effect
My car won't start, even after paying a repair bill of $500.	My car is reliable. The mechanic is competent, fair, and trustworthy. I paid $500 only three days ago to repair my car (present).	What do I instinctively do?	My anger, fear, or doubt (reaction). My laughter, patience, or curiosity (response). The experiences of other limitations imprinted in my brain (past).

If I accept "creative imagination," this happens: an outside event (a car that won't start) activates my inner pictures (my car is reliable, recently repaired). Underneath these pictures are other pictures of life's limitations from the past (mental shed). I may react before I respond: "I hate this car!" Or I may use the *stable* explanatory style: "I always have dumb luck." But once I get my bearings, another picture may emerge: "I wonder what happened?" There's another door, another opportunity, another choice. If my creative imagination elicits another picture, I break the conditioned response. I don't have to live underneath my picture and *react*. I can make a new *response*.

An exercise that can help you use the ideas from this chapter in your life is printed on page 118 in the exercises section in the back of the book.

2

Setting Yourself Up for Disappointment

You can, without being aware of it, arrange for your own frustration. One way involves your *beliefs*. Beliefs are mental pictures. Certain beliefs are "set ups" for disappointment, even despair. By believing the way you do, you prepare your own suffering.

Birth is the first frustration. Your separation from mother is a "terrible disappointment in love." Leaving the womb, you lose what developmental psychologists call the "steady state of bliss" and "oceanic feeling." As a fetus, "that happy period," you are are physically part of mother, receiving an endless stream of nutrients from her, such as food and oxygen. Suddenly the protective envelope is shed. Oneness ends abruptly. You feel hunger and discomfort. And you are exposed to change in temperature, light, and noise. "We begin with loss," Judith Viorst says in *Necessary Losses;* "We are cast from the womb without an apartment, a charge plate, a job or a car." You enter life as a stranger in a strange land with all the anxiety strangeness brings.

You enter the world complaining. Your first attempt at self-disclosure is crying. Wailing is your first public speech. Birth is the first of all the grievances in life. For the "birth trauma" is carried into every stage of life. The psyche never forgets.

Astrology, called "the first doctrine of the birth trauma," was an early attempt to deal with the crisis of loss and disappointment. It is based on what happens in the heavens at the moment of birth. Since everyone is born under the celestial stars, everyone is attached to the universe. Its adherents believe that cosmic order answers the terror of the "disappointment in love." Mother Nature replaces the birthing mother. No life is a pathless plot—the heavens assure it.

Ancient people turned not only to nature to ease "separation anxiety" but also to history. They developed "rites of passage" for the occasion of separation. Primitive ceremonies clustered around puberty, marriage, and death, the new year or season, the entry into adulthood. Still today, we observe marker events: birthday, graduation, anniversary, promotion, and retirement. And what more frequent rite of passage is commemorated than the morning cup of coffee, identifying the transition from sleep to consciousness?

People still defend themselves against the "birth trauma." To escape disappointment, some quietly mask their desires or deny their needs or expect too little. By doing this, they avoid putting themselves in the position of being rejected and feeling estranged. They remove themselves from the "terrible disappointment in love." But at the same time they distance themselves from a full life.

More apparent, though, are those who are letting their disappointments be known. "Why does man," asks Walker Percy in *The Message in the Bottle*, "feel so sad in the twentieth century?" The good life has been achieved; expectations have risen. Nevertheless, "everything is upside down," Percy observes, "people feeling bad when they should feel good." Many recognize this to be a new nameless problem; it is a feeling of discontent, of restlessness. Everywhere are complaints of unmet needs, disappointments in one's self and in others.

These impressions are supported by several studies. According to estimates, 20 million Americans suffer monophobia, a "marked fear of being alone," reports the American Psychiatric Association. Triggering the attacks of panic are events involving loss and disappointment: the illness of a relative, surgery, the death of a close friend, moving, or pregnancy. Then another 20% of the American population, it is estimated, grieves to the point of depression on a given day. One out of five of us is the sad sack roaming our streets.

If disappointment is so widespread, what forces contribute to it? We will examine several *personal* forces, how we set ourselves up for disappointment, how some beliefs we hold about ourselves arrange our griefs. We will look at three people—Don, who believes he is *worthy and acceptable;* Kent, the *strong and superior;* Karen, the *good and loving.* To protect against disappointment, they formed beliefs about themselves, only to experience a deeper kind of disappointment.

Worthy and acceptable

Don, a minister in his mid-40s, complained that he could not eat regularly or sleep soundly. Petty items agitated his marital relationship. He could not concentrate at work. If the telephone rang, he felt tiny white-hot pains bubble inside him.

A small group of malcontents had formed in the congregation Don served. The dissidents were vocal, yet would not encounter Don face-to-face. They faulted him for a lack of growth in membership. One woman, serving as the group's "switchboard," attempted to find other grievances against Don to strengthen their dispute with him.

During therapy, old ghosts from the clergyman's past left their graves. Don recalled his relationship with his father, who regularly pointed out Don's failures and mistakes. As a child, and even up to the present, Don received a minimum of praise and positive affirmation from his father. Don said, "If he hadn't been such a stubborn perfectionist. . . ." Although he excelled in music and public speaking, Don also revealed how inferior he felt as an adolescent because he did not excel in athletics. In college Don pursued academic excellence—but felt worthless despite his success. Don felt depressed frequently and hid it in silence.

At the beginning of his ministry, 20 years ago, Don *believed* that saying no to the requests of others constituted an act of treason on his part. To win the approval of others, he permitted them to take their "bite" out of him. He became the "Right Reverend Friendly"—compliant, pleasant, agreeable. Now suddenly faced with the criticism of the malcontents, Don's discontent grew as he could focus on little else than the opposition. He felt ashamed. Don easily discounted himself with stabs of self-disdain. His pain slipped out into tears.

Actually, the dissatisfied group included a handful of people, not a formidable segment of the congregation. As the behind-the-scenes griping intensified, Don's supporters resisted the complaining minority. The voices of support were hardly audible to Don, but he heard the disgruntled.

Don refused to acknowledge his own rankled feelings about their complaints and secrecy. How could Don say what he really felt and yet risk the loss of approval of others? How could he muster the courage to disclose his feelings, especially anger, and respond differently to threatening circumstances? Don did it by changing his beliefs (mental images) about himself.

Could Don, the minister, see himself angry? He suppressed the feeling, based on his belief that anger was the equivalent of not loving. Worse yet, Don believed that his anger would turn others away from loving him. Since Don depended on others to feel worthy and acceptable, if he expressed anger, wouldn't he threaten his security? Year after year, Don accepted, not himself, but the thousand daily insults to his dignity. Don believed that he could not be angry and be loved. Don feared people would abandon him if he expressed anger, a fear he stored in his mental shed based on his relationship with his father. Don did not *define* himself from within as worthy and acceptable. He permitted other people to do it. But, of course, when some treated him as unworthy and unacceptable, he felt powerless because he had given others the power to define who he was. As Bill Cosby says, he does not know what makes for success, only what creates failure—trying to please everyone.

Strong and superior

Kent, a 20-year veteran college professor, phoned me and insisted on an immediate appointment. He mentioned that he was "up to his neck with rage," and it was spilling everywhere. Kent came to see me a few days later, quite displeased that I had not seen him immediately. Self-sufficient since late adolescence, Kent both conducted himself as and considered himself to be strong and superior. When he was 17, Kent's parents died. An only child, he inherited his parents' sandwich shop. He operated the business, entered graduate school in economics, and married an attractive coed.

Shortly before Kent's visit a young colleague in his department had received a research grant, much to Kent's resentment. He regarded the young professor as his inferior. Also preceding Kent's call was an incident with a female student who said, "I hope *you* can understand your lectures, because I can't." Kent exploded, calling her "a campus whore." At home Kent lashed out at his two sons. Recognizing Kent's unfairness, his wife reprimanded him for his severe behavior.

Kent sadly stated, "I'm losing my grip. I'm losing it." Kent challenged me, "What are you going to do? Give me a handle!" He doused me with the hot water of his hostility. Finally I interrupted, telling him frankly that I experienced him as being self-righteous, insufferable, and obnoxious. He retreated to the door, shouting, "You're a fake!"

A week later Kent called again. He demanded another immediate visit. "My wife won't sleep with me," he complained, "and you haven't helped at all." I told him that I could schedule him in five days. He attacked with obscenities, finally relenting and pleading, "Please, I've got to smooth things out." We met five days later.

Kent appeared resigned. He stated that he was no longer "bullish" on life and like the economy he was in a period of "recession." I responded, saying, "A business recession is like a person's depression." He retorted, "Do you mean that all this explosiveness is a depression?"

For several weeks we explored his resistance to the thought of death and to the losses he was now experiencing. Death is a great equalizer. To Kent, who considered himself to be not an equal but a superior being, death was intolerable. Later Kent became aware of his prolonged anger toward his deceased parents, whom he believed abandoned him at 17. Thirty years later these feelings edged their way into his consciousness.

When you overvalue someone, or overinvest in something, as Kent with his self-image of strength and superiority, you are extremely vulnerable to disappointment. "The bigger they are, the harder they fall." But you fall for one reason: you climb. The higher your self-ideal, the harder is your struggle with reality. You set yourself up for a fall. In Kent's situation other people paid for his "debt." To feel strong and superior, he attacked his two sons. Even when he resolutely announced to make up the difference to those he offended, I suggested that his efforts might be seen as a play of strength. Casually I mentioned that he might want to extend "credit" and lower the "interest rate," giving something of himself and being a "soft touch" for awhile.

In Kent's mental shed there would always be a picture of strength and superiority. That's how he survived since the age of 17, guarding against feelings of abandonment. But the therapy sessions themselves were new experiences for Kent. He encountered his long-hidden fear of being left alone, the picture stored and covered in the corner of his mind. He chose to see himself in another way, as someone who could be vulnerable in caring even as he was strong and independent in himself. He increased his joy in living by accepting *both* his strength and his weakness. Kent's wife and sons found more joy living with him.

Good and loving

Karen pictured herself as good and loving. Beneath her consciousness Karen, too, had an idealized self—the "good fairy godmother." In her late 20s, Karen had married an ambitious salesman a year before I met her. Her husband, Alan, did not choose to be a salesman for unknown reasons. Extremely aggressive, Alan could sell hot chocolate in August in the tropics. Karen was truly his complement—submissive, supportive, sensitive.

Karen's supportive actions kept her fragile self-esteem together. Unknowingly, Karen intended to be the good parent she missed in her own life. Raised by her alcoholic, divorced mother, Karen had little contact with her natural father, even though he lived nearby. She substituted her helpfulness for her father's neglect, her steadiness for her mother's unreliability. Like supportive people, she gave too much away. Alan took advantage of her generosity. But Karen expected Alan to return to her what she gave to him, despite the fact that she seldom told Alan what she needed from him. She felt cheated and resentful. Cinderella, bereft of Prince Charming, resorted to the language of the dependent child—crying.

Alan came into my office and made his first sales pitch, saying, "If you can cure her, I don't care what the cost is." When I made the point that their conflict was grounded in how they interacted, Alan discounted it, "Like I said, help her and the price will be right."

Behind Karen's behavior stood a basic belief. If she would be good, affectionate, and generous, then others would give her a fair exchange. Her dependence on Alan for the equity only doubled her trouble. Whenever the exchange did not materialize, she felt rejected. Karen's "power" existed in her goodness. She did not stand up to Alan; Alan acted like he always had—aggressively. Karen had no way to help Alan avoid hurting her.

Karen needed to learn how to balance the new, "I want from you," with the old, "I will give to you." Alan had to learn how to give as well as take. Change came slowly. Alan still believed Karen was the only one with a problem, and she did too. Karen's new belief—asking is a fitting partner for giving—developed over a period of time. Her good and loving actions left her dissatisfied. She doubled her efforts which merely set her up for deeper disappointment. When she started to ask Alan for little things, such as calling her when he was out of town, helping her make supper once a week, and putting the top on the tube of toothpaste, Karen's belief-picture changed and her crying spells diminished. Deeply embedded mental images resist change. But when you take responsibility for the change, even little things make a difference. Karen's change of behavior brought about a change in her self-image.

Seeing the blind side

Worthy and acceptable, strong and superior, and good and loving are ideals, images, pictures, appraisals, beliefs. There are many other such beliefs: positive and optimistic, free and easy, holy and righteous, clever and shrewd, bold and decisive, hard and fast, high and mighty. They are one-dimensional. That means they are only a *part* of the picture, not the whole. One-dimensional beliefs are effective for one side of the story—sunshine beliefs fail on rainy days. Dark pictures are hardly appropriate for lighter moments. Don's belief of being worthy and acceptable collapsed under disapproval and anger. Kent's belief of being strong and superior declined with a young faculty member's achievement. Karen's belief of being good and loving drowned in her tears of dissatisfaction. But their unhappy souls forced them to see what their beliefs would not permit them to see before. They had set themselves up for disappointment with "one-eye" beliefs. When they were forced to open the other eye, their pictures changed. The value of disappointment, or any suffering, is the possibility of taking another look, viewing yourself from a different angle, opening the mental shed to a new picture.

"Seeing is believing." True. But many times *believing is seeing*. The brain functions in two ways—to let light in and to seal it off. It is not a neutral vessel. Old beliefs stand at the door of your mental shed. For example, Don let in the light of whatever confirmed his belief of being worthy and acceptable. The rest he sealed off. Notice, too, your own statements of *disbelief* when something upsets your mental pictures—"Oh, no!" "Are you sure!" "I can't believe it." Two things break the grip of the old beliefs guarding your mental shed and allow the light to come in: 1) Some new experience with emotional impact (Kent) or 2) a new behavior which contradicts your old one-eye belief (Karen).

An exercise that can help you use the ideas from this chapter is printed on page 119 in the exercises section.

3

Loosening the Grip of Wishful Thinking

A second set of pictures—your wishes—prepare you for frustration. Your longings become schemes for your own discontent. They are too "long"—beyond your reach or beyond reality.

If only

We live a lie. We fool ourselves, wishing that either someone would sweep us off our lonely feet or something would bring us a streak of luck or the bluebird of happiness. Our lies are many; if we had more time, or money, or another chance, we would be satisfied. If only others would love us, if only others would change, if only others would take care of us, then we would know pleasure. If only fate, the stars, destiny, an angel, a lover, a fairy godmother, a rich uncle, a sweepstakes ticket, an oracle, or some tea leaves would tilt in our favor, then we would be on top of our world.

We are lied to: promised miracles, false assurances, and distorted claims. We are told that we can become financially secure through five steps, happy within 90 days, and winners three times over. We hitch our wagon to a shining star—a celebrity, a pot of gold at the end of the rainbow, a best-selling book, a smiling figure with a map to the land of milk and honey. But the Grand Solution is the Big Lie!

A story from the town of Hemingway, South Carolina, highlights how deceit and wish intermingle. A 33-year-old woman with a feigned British accent seized upon the town's desire for an inexpensive health clinic. For seven months she became their new doctor and provided the town of 1200 people with low-cost medical care and loving kindness. Residents loaned her money and fed her. But she turned out to be an imposter. Attuned to their longings, the citizens were deaf to common sense and judgment. "She zeroed in on any weakness you had," one of the Hemingway residents reported, "she always told everyone what they wanted or needed to hear."

Magical thinking

Since childhood, we have believed in magic. We were taught that wishing could make things come true. Our parents trained us in magical thinking. There was Santa Claus, the Easter Bunny, the tooth fairy, and the "surprises" parents promised for being good. There was good magic: a four-leaf clover, a religious charm, and a full moon. And there was bad magic: fool's gold, black cats, and the number 13.

Magical thinking extends into adult life. As the Hemingway incident illustrates, we continue to believe "our ship will come in," and rainbows will bring good fortune. Half in jest, half in anticipation, we "knock on wood" and cross our fingers. We look to newly-elected political figures to work their wizardry. We change partners or locations in the enchanted hope that the next experience will fulfill our longings. Today, of course, television distorts reality: knotty problems are solved in 30 minutes; the good guys always win; deep questions are given superficial answers. Then the advertising industry bewitches us, too, promising security and happiness through a pill, a product, or a proverb.

But, magical thinking renders us less powerful and more dissatisfied. We make wishes rather than make changes. We begin our sentences with I *wish*, such as "I wish I could change." What we are really saying is "I can't." Statements about wishing are self-excusing whimpers. "I wish I could" means "I don't care enough" or "I'm not able to."

In the world of imaginary longing, life always has a way of coming out "right" or "better." Someone said that *fantasies* are *faultless*. Sticky situations become velvet; rough problems are sandpaper smooth. Fantasy allows our wishes to come true. The pain of unpleasant reality is put aside in the Disneyland of our mind. Fantasy is the white lie we tell ourselves in order to deal with our dark night. In fantasy we edit the script, create the plot, and cast the roles. We fool ourselves to get what we want.

Briar-patch learning

I know this legendary world. I live it. At times I demand it. I live the lie, hungering for the simple solution, faulting others for my own unhappiness, nursing my psychic wounds with pity, creating a "second world" in order to make reality bearable, and hoping that wishing it will change it. Instead of wrestling with painful truth, I concoct a self-made world of enchantment or am enticed by the enchantment of someone else. I have learned, neither willingly nor easily, that the truth lies closer to the reality expressed by Bonaro W.

Overstreet, who says in *How to Think about Ourselves* (New York—London: W. W. Norton and Company, 1948):

> Often in these times, beset by many counsels, we feel like people entangled in a briar patch while purveyors of wisdom shout in contradictory chorus, "Go back where you came from!" and "Go on to where you should be!" Push and tug as we may in our zeal to obey all good counselors at once, we find that the only way to go anywhere, backward or forward, is patiently to unhook one thorn after another *where we are.*

In a world of enchantment a magic helper will wave a wand and say, "Go back!" A second enchanter with cards up her sleeves, advises, "Go on!" Entangled in a patch of discontent, we rush to them, hoping they will draw our lucky number. We are susceptible to deception of this kind because we have for so long used it on ourselves. Overstreet cautions not "to jump to conclusions." When we are caught in the briars, patience serves us better than zeal, standing still more than leaping into the deep end, and honoring the thorns where we are rather than rushing off to the Land of Oz. If we change geography, whether backward or forward, we still take the briars with us.

Discontent is pain. Pain is a teacher; pain carries information. All pain wants attention and a *response*—"to unhook one thorn after another." Some realities we only learn "in a briar patch," in discontent. Our pain can make us wiser. Pain is a powerful burden that throws us off balance, at least until identified, dealt with, and unhooked. Discontent is a message, alerting us to what we would like to wish away. Yet it calls to us, "Come down into grief and feel it." Once acknowledged and accepted, pain loses its early advantage and its powerful edge. Instead of being possessed by it, we

can possess it. In place of investing energy to escape from
the briars, we can use our energy where we are in our patches
of pain to work through them patiently.

Life begins at 40

I am at midlife. This period of life is aptly called a "briar
patch." Indeed I am pulling out thorns. I am battling
changes—some painful ones. I have to redraw the over-
drawn dreams of the past. My wild hopes need to be set
within boundaries. The fantasies I packed in my baggage
for life's journey need to be adjusted according to the limitations discovered on the journey. Wishing on a star must
be replaced by working on a realistic plan. Some of my
illusions, of course, refuse adjustment. Illusions are like
death and taxes—always there. I cannot live without some
fictions, second worlds that repair the disappointments of
the first world of reality. Illusions repair what is torn and
bleeding; illusions dramatize and nourish a new reality. *They
negate the existence of conflict.* Temporarily, they relieve the
pain of discontent.

At this stage of life, I need to color my wishes with shades
of wisdom. I need to be honest with myself. The time comes
for checks and balances. I must deal with the roses *and* the
thorns, the longings *and* the limits, what might yet be *and*
what is. Not all wishes come true, but all bills come due.
Truly, life begins at 40 or thereabout. Midlife is the time
when we weigh our wishes in the scale of reality. Our picture-wishes, drawn and detailed over a long period of years,
need fresh color, revised lines, and new shapes. Yet, how
painful, as Sam Keen describes it in *Maps of Faith:* "At
eighteen the world is an oyster; at forty it has begun to clam
up. It takes immense courage and honesty to open it up and
turn it all into clam chowder."

The wish

Life without illusion would be unbearable, yet illusions create terrible anxieties. What are the midcourse corrections of our illusions? In the "briar patch" of midlife what are the thorns that need pulling? I offer several of my own as examples. The first thorn is myself, more accurately, my *idealized* self. For years I held a lofty self-perception about my ability to tolerate any type of personality. But my illusion collapsed. I came into frequent contact with an individual who would not reveal his anger but would take secret revenge with hostile jokes, only then to turn around and please me. When I confronted him about his behavior and my reaction to it, he said he was surprised, and claimed innocence. After repeated confrontations, he distanced himself. When reports of our rift became public, he acted as if all were well. I felt angry. At first, though, I thought my anger was solely a reaction to his behavior. Later I discovered that my anger was just as much related to the severe bruising of my idealized omnipotence: I could work with anyone. Behind my illusion was a simple wish to be Mr. Pleasant, to be a high-standing member of the party of A.G.O.B. (Alliance of Good Ole Boys).

A second thorn involved my first caretakers. I projected onto my parents a sense of perfection and invincibility. Any chipping away of my ennoblement of them met my resistance. I would not allow dents and cracks in my glorified image. My wishful thinking created blameless parents. In the last few years, I have become tolerant of their reality, even the truth of their limitations and insecurities. I have set my parents "free"—free from being godlike and magnified. Yet while I do this, I find no less respect and love for them. I love them, in fact, in a truer sense, for the persons they are, instead of for what I need from them. My fanciful notions provided me with a sense of security. I idealized my parents in order to protect myself. If they are imperfect, where does that leave me?

Wishing became apparent to me in another area—marriage. My wife and I lived a lie. We believed that our marriage would be happy for no other reason than we *wished* it. When it was not really blissful, we stashed away disappointment in the closet of silence. Confusing matters, we kept pretending:

"Someday this stress will quietly pass away in the night and delight will return."

"I'll be happy as soon as she decides to change."

"There's no hope for us. We'll just have to become satisfied with our dissatisfaction."

"My life will be better once he gets through this phase."

While we pretended all is fine, we acted in a way many do in their marriages. We "upped the ante." We demanded even more of one another. We wished for more without asking for it. We did "bad things" to get "good things" because the good things did not work magic anymore. Our discontent motivated change. We learned how to tell one another what we needed, how to express feelings more openly, and how to grant independence to one another and to our own selves. Less preoccupied with maintaining the illusion of happiness, we are reaching for the realities of living with imperfect selves and yet meeting our need for intimacy. We are changing our "pictures" of each other. Rather than wishing on the marital star, we are working on the reality of our relationship.

Yet another entanglement involved my four children. I destined them to achieve in my behalf the things which I could not achieve for myself. They would take up the slack of my deficiencies. One might call it the "Little League Syndrome," where parents seek vicarious fulfillment through their 12-year-olds. Another appropriate name might be the "Christmas Letter Complex" as parents write about their romance with their offspring—the second-grader headed for the NFL, the computer whiz, the princess, the wonder child, the world's next genius or celebrity. Each Christmas season children are given their "credentials," buttressing at the same time their parents' self-worth. It is a heavy load for children to bear responsibility for mother's happiness and father's pride. Laying a "trip" of happiness or pride on unprepared children is a form of counter-dependency. To expect our children to complete our wishes is an incredible illusion. It is a lie.

Truth and reality

We cannot live without illusions—imagined events that repair a disappointing world. And we never completely forsake the wish that discontent would stay out of our path forever. We wish the briars would fall out by themselves, or someone else would remove them for us. Wishes repair the unwished for, but they do not remove it. The moment of truth arrives when the tooth fairy no longer appears and the fabled rich uncle is evidently a ghost. Reality gets to speak its piece. Isn't this the significance of the remark in Walker Percy's *The Moviegoer*, where a character asks if "only in times of illness or disaster or death are people real." Such experiences shatter our picture-wishes and loosen the grip of wishful thinking. Truth has no respect for illusions; reality has no regard for our wishes.

Loosening the grip

Our lies, in the forms of wishes and illusions, protect us for a time and up to a point. We need "urgent lies" in order to escape the full onslaught of reality; we need the "rosy picture" when we are up to our necks in thorns. Making a wish is making life as pleasurable as possible. Two enterprising businessmen in Maryland, for example, have formed a company that offers fantasy tapes of major sporting events, placing the average person in the role of a hero. The two entrepreneurs say that the tapes help the ordinary person feel younger, special, like a star. "When people hear their names on the tapes," one of the company owners says, "they get a feeling of warmth and happiness." The tapes, he believes, give "people the opportunity to change things." What happens is not change, simply temporary repair. Wishing, pleasurable as it is, rewards us. What rewards becomes addictive. We become wishaholics.

The difficulty with the mental shed of wishes always is giving them up; the difficulty is breaking their grip. Using wishful thinking to control the forces and events of life, we may find that they begin to control us. We *wish* to be more content instead of *choosing* to be. We fall into the arms of "If-only":

If only this would happen . . .

If only you would help . . .

Or we embrace the "Whens":

When I get out of this situation . . .

When you change yourself . . .

Or we cling to the "What-ifs":

What if this changed . . .

What if I had not . . .

We deal with our discontent in seventh heaven, not *where we are*. Wishing cancels out responding. Whenever we place round illusions in the square hole of reality, we stand at the edge of hopelessness; contentment becomes only something we can wish for, but not choose.

The grip of wishful thinking prevents us from *grappling* with our experience. But strength comes from the struggle, from the school of reality. If we are conditioned to wishes and fantasies, we never discover courage. And we cannot live our best lives telling lies, M. Scott Peck observes in *People of the Lie,* and, I would add, accepting the lies we are told. Liars are the least courageous people.

Take, for instance, the parents of a teenage daughter who has suffered brain damage in an automobile accident. Slowly they realize that they lost the daughter they once had—a painful truth. Her beaming personality and vitality cannot be restored. They remember how she was before and at the same time face the irreversible reality of who she is now. But their daughter's struggle to live, just to communicate again, becomes the parents' new hope. They do not abandon her because she is no longer who she was. They care for her so that she might be more than a helpless shell of flesh and bone. She will never go to college, marry, or have children. Those wishes are gone. But that she might be able to talk, to learn her identity, or to regain a few basic skills, these become the new pictures, the sources of hope. Overcoming their defensiveness about what happened, the parents discover the strength to be responsive to what is. They reframe the picture of their wishes. Certainly they settle for "less." But they do not settle for nothing. Their hope is grounded in a new reality, a new picture. Their hopes are smaller, nonetheless, their courage is greater. Refusing magic, they learn the hope made real in little things for their daughter. Loosening the grip of wishful thinking, they love her, as only love can, as she is and might yet become.

An exercise that can help you use the ideas from this chapter in your life is printed on page 120 in the exercises section.

4

Finding the Missing X

Together with beliefs and wishes, expectations prepare the way for discontent. Certainly expectations excite and energize. They lift the ceilings of life. When unrealistic or exaggerated, expectations lead you to the dead end of disappointment.

Questions, cravings, strivings

Something is missing.

Your life is confusing. There is a missing X. A Mercedes? A religious experience? Something your parents never had? Maybe even the key to the universe?

You need something to feel complete. Could it be a second career? A perfect lover? Money? A miraculous cure?

You feel anxious and driven. You expect more or something else than this. Success? A change of scenery? Companions?

Gaps and holes exist in your experience. Not sure of everything, you question. Being a limited creature, you crave attachment to someone or something. Not at home everywhere, you push forward. Something is missing. Out of your quest for the secret X, your expectations emerge. You live on the edge of the present, pursuing a second chance, a heaven on earth, a big break, a bit of magic, a deep fulfillment, a happy ending. Your expectations are pictures in your head: pictures of something new, something different, something better.

The missing X, once found, does not always meet the promise you make in its name. The missing X may turn out to be a 0. "The open road," the poet warns, "leads to the used car lot." In your frantic pursuits, you mistake what is probable for what is possible. Expectations are positive, moving forces, but they have a dark side, an underside—especially if you live *underneath* them.

Three types of expectations create dissatisfying results: expecting too little, expecting too much, and expecting something else, "anything but this."

Expecting too little

Some people trim their expectations to ground level. Their mental pictures are mini-size. Having experienced deep, painful disappointments in the past, they now defend themselves against the disappointment again. They expect too little.

A turtle family went on a picnic. They had prepared seven years for their outing. The family left home searching for a suitable place. During the second year of their journey, they found it. For about six months they cleared the area, unpacked the picnic basket, and completed the arrangements. They discovered, however, that they had forgotten the salt. A picnic without salt would be a disaster, they all agreed. After a lengthy discussion, the youngest turtle was chosen to retrieve the salt at home. Although he was the fastest of the slow-moving turtles, the little turtle whined, cried, and wobbled in his shell. He agreed to go only on the condition that no one would eat until he returned. The family consented. The little turtle left.

Three years passed—but the little turtle did not return. Five years. Six years. Then in the seventh year of his absence, the eldest turtle could no longer contain his hunger. He announced that he was going to eat and began to unwrap a sandwich. At that point the little turtle suddenly popped out from behind a tree, shouting, "See, I knew you wouldn't wait; now I'm not going to get the salt."

Some kind of "little turtle" exists in you; you expect the worst! But negative expectations have a purpose—to prevent disappointment. Ground-level expectations defend you against shock, shame, or sadness. Several varieties of the "See, I knew you wouldn't wait" defense against disappointment are noted below:

Negative Expectation	Real Want
(1) "She will never love me."	(1) "I want her to love me."
(2) "He won't change."	(2) "I want him to change."
(3) "They'll choose someone else."	(3) "Please choose me."
(4) "Everything goes against me."	(4) "Give me a break."

Fearful of disappointment, you may become a chronic complainer, a "crybaby." "I never get a chance; I never get invited." Before anything ever happens, the chronic complainer will expect rain to fall on *every* parade and *always* on the day of a picnic. They know beforehand that they will have the worst time, the worst seat, and the worst job. "It *never* fails; it *always* happens to me." These people collect grievances to defend themselves against dissatisfaction of a deeper kind, using the global explanatory style.

The chronic complainer, who we know is not much fun to live with, is a passive victim achieving hollow victories through whining. Let me introduce you to William, a perennial pouter.

"I married below myself. I could have done better. My wife is sort of a loser."

"No, I'm not going to vote today. My candidate will lose anyway."

"My mother, I remember, used to tell me that 'dreams are for fools.' "

"I doubt if you are going to help me. All the others failed."

"I can't help it if I'm critical. I was born that way."

"Why go through all that trouble? No one will appreciate it."

"My wife says that I'm too negative. You know what? She's right. You'll never see me go down without a complaint."

William degrades his friends, accuses others, and protests against almost everything. He expects too little—and gets what he expects. William resembles the man who put his nose in limburger cheese only to come up and to announce, "The whole world stinks!"

William is the first one to tell you, "You can't do it." And if you don't, he's the first one to remind you, "See, I told you so." William expects negative things to happen. He carries discontent in his back pocket, or more precisely, in his fearful, small soul. William's trouble is not that he is a pessimist or a negative thinker, or for that matter a monstrous bore. William's problem begins with his expectation: something will always be missing. Poor William! Possessing a small picture of the world, he chooses the "victim mentality." William spends his lifetime defending against disappointment. Gray yesterday, cloudy today, and tomorrow will be more of the same. William's public groans protect him from private sorrow. Since he has been painfully hurt before, William will not risk much, lest the old feelings return. Instead of making changes in himself, he moans about everything else.

Expecting too much

Expecting too little is unrealistic—a distortion of reality. But expecting too much is a kindred exaggeration, just as much a defense against real sorrow. No matter what happens, the incurable romantics find sweetness and light, bluebirds and moonbeams, happy days and rich possibilities. They bury their fear of disappointment under the glow of optimism and good cheer. To all outward appearances, they are well-adjusted, well-liked, and full of confidence. They always see pink elephants. Reality never seems to sober them up. Life is roses, chocolates, and money in the bank.

"Think positively!"

"Look for the bright side!"

"Smile!"

These happy innocents are intoxicated with possibility. Think it! Watch it happen! Presto! Abracadabra! Positive thinking is strong motivation. It is one way of expressing your power, your responsibility for yourself. But it is a form of magical thinking—you cannot control every event of life with your mind. Not only is this arrogant, but also it is *defensive*. The builders of the tower of Babel were the greatest of positive thinkers. But their motivation was defensive. "Come, let us build ourselves a city, with a tower that reaches to the heavens, so that we may make a name for ourselves and not be scattered over the face of the whole earth" (Genesis 11:4).

Bert is an incurable romantic. When he came to see me, he looked cheerful and at ease. Bert's tranquil mood caught my attention immediately. He apologized for taking up my time. "I know you see the sick and the crazy," he stated calmly, "the negative types." Then he assured me that he was not one of them. In a matter of fact manner, Bert sketched out "a little conflict" he was having at work, interspersing comments about his confidence in resolving it. I knew Bert was more concerned with making a favorable impression on me than offering an honest expression of himself. I wondered to myself whether Bert would allow anyone to disturb his camouflage. What Bert described as "a little conflict" actually involved a major resentment of him by his coworkers. Innocently, Bert expected those who opposed him to act eventually in Bert's interest. He expected them to take clues from his positive attitude rather than from their own resentful feelings and negative perspectives. He had tied a yellow ribbon around his life.

After several visits Bert told me that his best friend had betrayed him with a campaign of "dirty tricks." He had been asked to resign his position at work. I could detect no sorrow. Still, Bert exuded confidence and cheerfulness. Once again I wondered if I would ever be able to help him push aside all the balloons, all the streamers, all the confetti—the bright optimism hiding his grief. He smiled his depression; he swallowed his anger; he numbed his wound. Optimism was Bert's perceptual anesthesia and he went his way in life before I found out if he ever came out of it.

Incurable romantics refuse to accept negative thoughts and unwanted feelings. Sadness is forbidden territory. Bert would let nothing affect his great expectations. But he was just as much a victim as his counterpart, William, the chronic complainer. By overlooking the ugly reality of betrayal, Bert unknowingly gave it immense power.

Whatever you hide, conceal, or repress returns with vengeance. Your coverups are tacit evidence that what is hidden is threatening, too overwhelming for you. At the same time you lose the capacity and the nerve to respond to the unexpected, the unwanted, the reality at hand. Incurable romantics may not be "crybabies" like William and his kind, but they certainly are not "grown-ups." They are innocent children, thinking everything will come up roses for no other reason than they *think* it. They expect too much.

Expectations determine a person's reaction to the daily news. Newspaper readers frequently write letters to the editor bemoaning the amount of bad news reported. They ask why the newspapers don't report the thousands of good things happening around us each day. One such reader suggested that the news media not always wallow in the dirt but come up to smell the roses. Yet the *ordinary* is not news. The news consists of the *unexpected*. Honesty is only news in the context of lying and fraud. Not the thousands of good judgments, but the poor decisions make the headlines. Not the marriages that succeed, but the troubled ones receive attention. The news appears overwhelmingly negative because people expect things to be positive. Expecting too much, it is no wonder that we read news that sounds so bad.

M. Scott Peck reports that people ask him why there is evil in the world. Peck responds in *People of the Lie:* "It is as if we automatically assume this is a naturally good world that has somehow been contaminated by evil." He contends that the mystery of goodness is far greater than the mystery of evil. There are more reasons to *expect* the bad than the good.

The automatic expectation of the good is the inner picture of the incurable romantic, supported by many of our cultural myths of the American dream, the success story, the land of opportunity, and the "can do" spirit. Novelist John Cheever, quoted in *Is That All There Is*, says that the primary emotion of "the adult . . . American who has had all the advantages of wealth, education, and culture is disappointment." And Laurence Peter, author of *Why Things Go Wrong*, mentions: "Americans tend to be malcontents. No matter what they have, they want more."

We expect our questions to have answers, our cravings to find sweet satisfactions, and our strivings to lead to desired destinations. If there's a missing X, we'll find it, solve it, conquer it, or buy it. We expect a lot—stellar report cards from our children, lower taxes from our government, a winning season from our alma mater, fixes from our healers, and slim waistlines from our diets. We are bound for glory and, according to Cheever's and Peter's observations, for disappointment. Our picture of rising expectations blind us to earthly limits. In the process we lose touch with little things, personal things, and deeper things—things that count—all for the sake of a bunch of X's. Our mental pictures in the form of expectations are overblown, beyond what we can reasonably experience.

The glow of elsewhere

The chronic complainer expects *too little;* the incurable romantic expects *too much.* Between the two stands the anxious soul who expects *something different.* Real life is not here, not this. It is elsewhere. Physicists use the word *elsewhere* for realms of existence that we can imagine but cannot inhabit. *Elsewhere* is a world beyond human existence, something we can picture but not experience. *Elsewhere* has a glow and a magnetism. In the movie, "Lovers and Strangers," a son tells his father that he and his wife of a few years have decided to divorce because, as he puts it, "We feel there must be something more." The father answers, "We all feel there must be something more." To which the son replies, "Then why don't you leave mom and go out and get it, dad?" The old man yells back, "Because there isn't something more!"

More, more, more! It's our picture of life. Richard Louv in his book, *America II*, compares the American dream to an "image of elsewhere." During the 18th and 19th centuries, America, the land of opportunity, had a "glow," and many of our ancestors had anxiety. There was gold in the hills and riches under the earth. You could make hay or grow it. And you could always stretch the dream by going west. Then, centuries later, you could have a two-acre spread 10 miles out of town or a condo with a marina in the center of the city, your own business, early retirement, two cars in every garage, and a chicken in every pot, a new Garden of Eden where each had a slice of God's acreage connected by the interstate highway system and major airlines. More importantly, the expectation of something different, once space and fortune, turned to the "self." New expectations of self-fulfillment emerged. Instead of going west, people went into themselves for the mysterious X, the something else.

Finding it

The glow of elsewhere brought Judy and her husband Steve to counseling. Judy represented the new breed of uneasy seekers. Over a period of nine months, Judy became aware of her uneasiness, which sometimes broke out into fiery complaints and at other times collapsed into eerie silence. Twenty-six years of marriage. Two children in college. A 12-year career. Suddenly—uneasiness! As Judy realized her many unmet needs, she brooded, and she blamed. Occasionally she shifted into self-blame for allowing her accumulated needs to continue untouched. Most of the time, she spilled it on her husband and her children. Steve, seeing how restless and resentful she had become, attributed it to the "empty nest," the crisis of midlife, and other reasonable causes. And yet the longer Judy expressed her discomfort, the more frightened and confused her husband became.

Judy announced that she wanted to "find it," but she could not specify what "it" was. All she knew, Judy exclaimed, was that "it" was not "this." For years Judy lived the role of supermom—the obsessive-compulsive caretaker. Many needs suffocated under the weight of her overfunctioning. Now her denied needs started to rumble like a volcano, ready to take vengeance for prolonged neglect. She felt deprived. She yearned for something more, elsewhere. As Judy's inner revolution stirred, the missing X compelled her. She was extremely susceptible to the *glow*. Her expectation of finding "it" became as obsessive as her caretaking. Judy prepared herself to compensate somewhere else for her long-ignored needs. She refused to acknowledge her own conspiracy in the denial of her needs; she denied responsibility for what she felt. But as Gertrude Stein noted— "there is no there, there."

Mental pictures of Fantasy Island or Wonderland may temporarily relieve our disappointment. But once blinded by the glow of elsewhere, we suspend our awareness and judgment. We expect contentment to be somewhere else, not somewhere within ourselves. To expect elsewhere to do for us what we refuse to do for ourselves is to escape from responsibility. Nevertheless, every *elsewhere* will be tested, even as each *here* is tested. What is now glowingly different becomes the eventual, unsparkling "same old thing." And then we will need another glow to snatch us from our discontent.

Eager longing is not our problem; it gives energy and inspiration. When incomplete, we naturally expect something else. But desperate longing is precisely what creates the *brightness* of elsewhere. We redden the glow because of our own shadowy selves. The luster of something different stands in proportion to our own dullness. "Anxiety," warns Gregory Bateson in *Step to an Ecology of Mind*, "creates its own disaster." Here, there, or elsewhere! Emptiness, not fullness, sharpens the glow.

Discontent is our lot, our property, our guilt. And contentment, that abundance of human spirit, is ours as well. What we seek elsewhere is to be found inside. It is not what enters the heart from the outside that corrupts, but what comes from the heart. Likewise it is not what is outside that brightens life, but what comes from within. The missing X is found in the unfolding of the self.

An exercise that can help you use the ideas from this chapter is printed on page 121 in the exercises section.

Part Two

How You Deal
with Your Discontent

5

Taking a
Psychological Bath

Blaming is one means to purge frustration. You fault others or circumstances for what you are responsible. You want to feel good rather than bad, clean instead of dirty, and right in contrast to wrong. Discontent hurled at someone or something through blaming is self-defense. But there is no self-understanding. By blaming you excuse yourself from the need to change and place the need somewhere outside yourself.

Gripes and goats

Cleanliness is next to godliness. The next time you get into a conflict, after the smoke and dust have cleared, examine what happened. You will notice that a good part of the argument was based on your eagerness to prove that you were right, to purify yourself. The bitter and unhappy parts, you will recognize, were due to your need to justify yourself. "You do it your way; I'll do it God's way."

Griping at someone, you use "smear tactics." You are not above "foul play" or "doing one dirt" when you argue vehemently. In the heat of a contest, you "muddy up the waters" and "cloud up the issues." All this is done in the name of innocence, purity, and goodness. There is great truth in G. K. Chesterton's remark: "I like to get into hot water; it keeps me clean." As much as you dislike conflict, you feel that you need it. You get into hot water because you want to be clean, to be next to godliness. Your battles with others involve more than winners and losers or who is strong and who is weak. Conflict can also be seen as a matter of goodness or badness. It's a matter of wanting to feel clean.

Consider the many words referring to *cleanliness* we use to describe the outcome of competitive games:

Reds *soak* Giants;

Vikings *polish off* Rams;

Tennessee *routs* Alabama;

Republicans *sweep* Democrats;

North *mops up* South.

If a candidate is defeated for a third or fourth time, the oft-defeated is "washed up." When a team fails to score, we call them the victim of a "whitewash." A player removed from a game is said to be "sent to the showers." Losers are "taken to the cleaners" or "put through the wringer." Any disappointment can be called a "washout."

Conflicts are messy. But you want to leave the fracas clean, with your self-image presentable. To accomplish this, you convert your griping into scapegoating. A scapegoat is someone who is set up for taking the blame. In the Yom Kippur ceremony, a he-goat, upon whose head are placed the sins and guilt of the people, is sent into the wilderness. The goat carries away the people's evil. Hence medieval witchcraft personified the devil as a goat. Today we label the individual who commits an untimely mistake "the goat."

The more you need to be right, the more the conflict becomes a "holy war," an attempt to be on the side of the angels and saints. Wanting to be good and clean, you address your opponent, "You dirty devil." Furthermore, you can always blame the evil forces themselves: "The devil made me do it."

To rid yourself of blame, you send out "you messages." A husband accuses his wife: "You never think of anyone but yourself." Reacting quickly, she censures him for paying too much attention to his friends and neglecting her. The President faults Congress; Congress countercharges. "You! You! You!" If someone's belly is aching acutely, someone else's head will roll accordingly. Assigning guilt back and forth, you play the "hot potato game." You make a martyr of the other, if not a fool of yourself. You insist on being the "nice girl" or the "good boy." Gripes give birth to goats.

Emotional housecleaning

You discharge discontent by laying blame. You appoint people, groups, or situations to serve as bellhops to carry away your baggage of displeasure. You are ready to use anyone as a target. Even substitute scapegoats will do. Instead of confronting your boss with whom you are angry, you blast your horn at motorists on the way home. Arriving safely home, you still "kick the cat." You can only wonder how many times your children have had to pay for someone else's debt. Unfortunately, you take out your frustrations on those who are closest to you.

Recently I saw a bumper sticker that said: "To err is human. To blame is even more human." When you feel displeased, vulnerable, or helpless, you throw your feeling onto the lap of someone or something. You don't like these feelings, and you don't want to be responsible for them. Not able to tolerate something in yourself, you condemn it in another. You *project*. A drunken driver kills a family of four; he blames the bartender who served the drinks. A husband physically abuses his wife; he blames his cold mother. A child drops out of school; he blames his teachers. A woman suffers a great loss, only to blame God.

In the following statements, notice how negative feelings are disowned:

John: "*You* make me sick."

Mary: "*You* cause my unhappiness."

John: "*You* started this mess."

Mary: "Well, *you're* no angel."

John and Mary are engaged in emotional housecleaning. Their comments begin with *you*. What actually rests within John is blamed on Mary, and what belongs to Mary is placed on John. John disowns his "sick" feelings, and Mary disavows her "unhappy" feelings. John and Mary turn what is felt inside into something outside themselves. They place the need for change in the other.

What do John and Mary accomplish? Let's use John as the example.

John feels *superior* by designating Mary as the culprit of his negative, unwanted feelings.

John *protects* his self-worth from injury.

John *rejects* responsibility for his own discontent.

John uses blaming to make an issue *perfectly clear* in his own mind.

As John *scours* his soul, he *scrubs* Mary. Meanwhile Mary *polishes* her image of herself as she *dumps* on John. When they get into hot water, both John and Mary try to get clean. But each one sees the other as an image, a container, an object. They no longer relate to one another as *persons*. Their projections distort their partners.

Blame and shame

You disown a fault, a feeling, or a failure. You put it *out there*. How convenient! Now you can go about your business feeling worthy, pure, and clean. Blaming is taking a psychological bath. "I'm clean. You are at fault."

In the story of Adam and Eve, God confronts the couple after they violate the command about eating the fruit of the tree. Adam says to God: "The woman you put here with me—she gave me some fruit from the tree, and I ate it." Then it's Eve's turn and she says, "The serpent deceived me, and I ate." Neither one acknowledges responsibility for their own action. They do not deny their eating; they deny their responsibility for it. Adam and Eve present themselves to God as innocent victims. By scapegoating, Adam blaming Eve, and she the serpent, they keep their slate clean.

The story introduces a connection between blame and shame. Naked, they clothe themselves. Afraid, they hide themselves from the presence of God. Adam and Eve feel disgraced, exposed. Rather than face their shame, they hide; shame is a powerful, painful feeling. It spreads through your whole body and eventually reveals itself in blushing. Humans are the only animal that becomes red-faced in shame. Humans never blush in solitude but always in the presence of another person. Thus you speak about "hiding your face in shame" or being "shamefaced" and "I can't face him" or "I couldn't stand to look her in the eye."

Ralph Keyes wrote a book about taking risks (*Chancing It: Why We Take Risks*). He discovered a link between taking risks and feeling shame. He said, in fact, that we will "risk life before dignity." We'll take the chance of losing our body before we'll take the chance of losing our face. Keyes attributes risk taking to the avoidance of humiliation more than to the satisfaction of sensation.

The strength of shame is evidenced in its use as punishment. Closely knit groups employ the practice of "shunning" to dishonor an offender of community standards. Years ago, placing a wayward character in stocks was an acceptable form of public shaming, as were whippings, hangings, and dunkings. In the last century, dueling was still an acceptable practice for defending your honor and restraining shame. After the pardon of former President Richard Nixon, many defended the decree, believing the humiliation he suffered for Watergate and his resignation were due punishment.

In conflict you add *insult to injury*. You *blame* and *belittle*. Conflict is a "dirty shame." "You are at fault! Shame on you!" The more shame you heap upon your adversary, the purer and more godly you may feel. Even the everyday putdown, the petty nagging, the nitpicking, the whining, and the exaggerated complaint are attempts to be clean. You feel like you have just finished a hot bath and you think you have cleansed your soul.

Conflict includes blaming and shaming. You "throw dirt." You accuse. To ensure your purity, you also "dig up dirt." You ridicule your opponent. At the same time you project onto others and you pull them down.

Blaming	Shaming
(1) You *project* unwanted feelings of your own onto a target.	(1) You create *distance* between yourself and another by claiming goodness for yourself and badness in another.

(2) You *attribute* to others thoughts, feelings, or actions that belong to you.

(2) You *defend* against your feelings through the exposure of the other's badness.

(3) You *credit* to someone a dark characteristic, a forbidden desire, or an undesirable trait that belongs to you as belonging to them.

(3) You *keep* the other in the role of "goat" whose evil is great.

(4) You *order* your world by fixing blame, gaining a sense of control.

(4) You *relinquish* responsibility for what is happening when the other is so shamefully pictured.

(5) You *preserve* your self-image—dignified, righteous, and clean.

(5) You *set up* the other for the negative you expose about them.

You handle discontent by purging yourself of it—blaming and shaming others. But your inner wounds are not healed by placing them outside yourself.

Coming clean

Psychology and religion meet in their judgment of self-deception, the denial of responsibility, and the escape from reality. "The psyche, like truth," writes Alan McGlashan in *Gravity and Levity*, "is comfortable only when naked." And William Stringfellow adds that the demonic is disabled only through exposure ("Biography as Theology," *Katallagete*, Winter 1981). As a way of avoiding the nakedness and the exposure, you scapegoat and pour shame on others. In your need to feel clean, to see yourself as faultless, you sacrifice others. To sustain your dignity, you lay blame but do not establish responsibility. You discredit someone instead of taking ownership for yourself. Coming clean is neither a natural nor a simple process. Confession may be good for the soul, but it is not good for the face. What does it profit you if you gain your *face* but lose your *soul*?

So mental health workers and spiritual leaders advocate self-disclosure, accepting your torn and bleeding parts which before appear unworthy of the best definition of who you are. Paradoxically, you blame and shame to evade self-disclosure. Yet both are forms of self-disclosure. You are afraid of being found imperfect, incomplete, impure—not "right." In blaming and shaming, you disclose that you are not sure of your goodness. The story of Sara depicts this irony.

The princess and the gypsy

Sara is a middle-aged woman who for years has blamed her family for her own series of misfortunes. Pregnant at 30, she married a man with whom she shared no significant emotional bonds. After three years of intermittent struggle and threat, Sara abandoned him and their child. She left town and found a job in the Southwest only to go through several relationships that failed as miserably as her marriage. She maintained minimal contact with her younger sister, whom she detested, resenting her for being her parents' favorite child. Her random correspondence with her parents consisted of brief information and scolding. Sara took those as opportunities to take a psychological bath, scorning her parents for rejecting her by favoring her sister. Her two visits with her family, one day events in a period of seven years, left her feeling more empty and bitter than before. She would not let go of her gripes and goats.

Sara had given immense power to her *past*. She could not enjoy the present or plan for the future. What she wanted desperately from her parents, acceptance and affection, she could not give to herself or to others. After a year in therapy,

Sara began to deal with some exposure and truth. She recognized at last, although she did not feel it, that she tried to cleanse herself of her negative feelings by blaming her parents. Sara resented them for courting and crowning her younger sister, "the princess." The truth of the matter, though, was that Sara yearned to be the royal offspring and envied her sister. Sara detested being Cinderella's sister. When Sara admitted that her pregnancy, failed marriage, other broken relationships, and geographical distance from home were her attempts to get attention from her parents, as well as to get revenge, she loosened her hostile feelings. "I became the vagabond—the gypsy," she said softly, "because I could not be the princess." She smiled. And she cried. "You are telling me," she said as she dried her tears, "that I made a choice . . . my behavior was my choice . . . and all this time I not only wanted to hurt them . . ." She stopped. More tears. "I wanted them to love me too."

Sara tried to get the good things she wanted from her parents by being bad, then blaming her badness on her family. Deep in her heart, stashed away in her unconscious, embedded under layers of hostility, she still yearned for her childhood dream, to be the princess.

Sara was fortunate. Her spiritual community lended her their hope. They cared for her; they accepted her. In a sense, they reparented her. She discovered that forgiveness involved more than feeling better about her past. Forgiveness gave her back her future. She could start afresh. As Sara confessed the ugly, passionate, and bleeding parts of herself, she needed less of her blaming to save face. "God's forgiveness," she said, "has opened up my life . . . the scars of the past are there but I have a future." Sara began to call her parents, talking openly about her long-time feelings of rejection. She chose to be responsible for her feelings and her tomorrows. Decreasing her psychological baths, she needed the role of the gypsy less and less. After her break-through of many months, she visited her parents and sent me this letter:

Dear Pete,
   We hugged and kissed and cried. I feel closer to them. Not as close as I would like to feel. But close. Never did I think that I would do it. Oh, I was nervous. But I acted on your suggestions. I asked my mother to take me shopping and to buy me something. My dad (I think he thought I was crazy), held and rocked me when I asked him. This would not have happened if I had not had time to grieve, to look at myself. My mad impulse to lay blame—well, it's there in my mind. But I'm aware of it. I can do something about it. Oh, yes, I did enjoy being the child, the shopping and the rocking.
                                        Love,
                                        Sara

P.S. "No one who puts his hand to the plow and looks back is fit for the Kingdom of God" (Luke 9:62).

An exercise that can help you use the ideas from this chapter in your life is printed on page 122 in the exercises section at the back of the book.

6

Who Said Life Was Fair?

A common way to deal with discontent is to *brood*. Since you believe, wish, or expect life to be fair, you feel offended when it is not. To defend against the unfairness, you sulk and pout. Some, instead, *banish* the unfairness from their consciousness. There is a gravitational pull toward blotting out the displeasure from the mind in numbness. Either way, your discontent grows out of proportion to the reality of things.

A missing piece

Carl is a successful executive. At the mid-century mark of life, he is pleased with his circumstances, in excellent health, and optimistic about the future. His two children are on their own and doing fairly well; his wife Debra has started her own small business. Listening to Carl speak of his overall contentment, I wondered what led him to make an appointment for counseling. "I've been reading a couple of surveys lately," he reported, "the ones about satisfaction and happiness." Not surprisingly, Carl included himself in the high group who report 80% or more satisfaction with their lives. The remaining percentage, Carl's dissatisfaction, centered around his work, more specifically, his supervisor.

"You wouldn't believe what this guy does to me, and he gets away with it." As Carl unravelled several events, he spoke with hard resentment. "I can't look at him—maybe a glance and a hollow hello. When I see that he's out of the office for the day, my whole day is different . . . I mean different." Since Carl's work played a significant part in his life, the 20% unhappiness loomed larger than the figure would indicate. Carl mentioned that he was considering a change of jobs. "You get to a place where most of the pieces fit," Carl brooded, "but one thing throws you off balance." When I interrupted Carl's complaints about his boss, trying to move him to his feelings of anger, Carl stubbornly returned to the chief executive officer's behavior. Carl believed that if this one annoyance would be removed from his life, then he would be content. Carl's 20% discontent had a power greater than its percentage, though he was not aware of it.

Ann, a 35-year-old teacher and wife of a minister, experienced similar feelings. An only child, Ann found herself in the middle of her parents' conflict. They had separated. Each appealed to Ann for sympathy and for support of their grievances against the other. Her own sense of contentment was high. But for six months she endured her parents' skirmishes and attempts to manipulate her.

She felt grief over the separation, anger with her parents' attempts to win her favor, and guilt for feeling angry with them since both were suffering. When she came to see me—complaining of low energy and general nervousness—she too expressed how unfair life could be. "I have a caring husband, two growing children, and a teaching job which is more satisfying than my two previous positions. But this . . . I just want it to go away—evaporate, disappear, resolve itself."

The relative weight

Carl and Ann represent people who, for the most part, have control over their lives, have attained some level of success or comfort, and have realized a measure of self-acceptance. But one fierce irritation nags at their overall sense of contentment. When the emotional impact is deep, the grinding issue far exceeds its actual weight. The 20 percent dissatisfaction becomes preoccupying, oppressive, and out of proportion to the whole situation. It is similar to doing four things well and making only one mistake. The 4-1 ratio is impressive. Nevertheless the one mistake triumphs over the four successes. One forgets the positive "4," because he or she is unwilling to accept the mistake of "1."

The significant factor is not the ratio between satisfaction and dissatisfaction, such as Carl's 80/20 division. The central issue is the emotional weight of either one. Carl's disappointment distracted him. Carl felt angry even when everything to a major degree was going well. How could he appreciate his many contentments despite one nagging disappointment?

Discontent is destructive when it grows out of proportion to the whole. Just how discontented or contented you are with life is largely a matter of how you perceive your situation. You may demand a better playing hand and want the cards reshuffled. Resenting an intrusive annoyance, wishing for a new deal, or wanting to be a person living some kind of perfect life, you approach life with a clenched fist. But what senseless suffering you endure, trying to make everything fit. Suffering is one thing, but crying away what contentments you do have is another thing.

At times life is not fair. It can be a riddle wrapped inside a puzzle; it can be random and haphazard. "Why this? Why now? Why me?" But do you want to let it dribble away, insisting this or that should not happen to you? "That's unfair; that's too disturbing; that's too much; that's not enough." If you allow the missing piece to control you because it is unacceptable and upsetting, you can forfeit the pleasant parts of life. Like Sophie in William Styron's novel, *Sophie's Choice*, you complain about "the unearned unhappiness." But it happens!

Regardless of what the ratio of satisfaction to dissatisfaction may be—80/20, 60/40, or 50/50—the shaded portion, that is, the discontent, can be the focus of great attention and energy. When it overwhelms you, the discontent darkens the 80, 60, or 50 percent to the point that these satisfactions are not affirmed, celebrated, or remembered. They lose their power. Wanting it all, you lose the portion of contentment you have. Throwing a clenched fist at the 20 percentage points of discontent, you lose something of the 80 percent.

The imbalance

Mary-Lou Weisman, writing for *The New York Times*, puts this "out-of-proportion" problem into a humorous commentary ("Couples Vie for 'Best Marriage' Honors," *The Dallas Morning News*, Dec. 28, 1983):

It is the sickening sense that everybody is having a better marriage than you are. It is the same fantasy that tempts people to believe that everybody else's Thanksgiving dinner was catered by Norman Rockwell, and that only you have a father who can't carve, a mother who can't cook, a divorced sister, a daughter who is having Thanksgiving with her boyfriend's family, an uncle who won't shut up about his sensitivity training, and no dog Spot. It is the same ultimately self-abusing urge that makes people cling to the fantasy—against all contrary evidence—that other people eat as much as they want. Only you have to diet.

Finding that glaring flaw, that one mishap, or that single unhappy circumstance, you inflate it. You enlarge it in proportion to your panic. You allow a slice of dissatisfaction to become two slices, three slices, half the pie. Brooding is a sign that your disappointment is swelling.

The forgotten

If not brooding, then banishing may become a means to deal with discontent. If Carl, for example, conceals his anger and dissatisfaction, he would have to pretend being completely contented. Carl would please his supervisor, cloaking his dislike under good cheer. But Carl's repressed feelings will be channeled somewhere else. They won't simply dissolve because they are repressed. Here are some possible consequences of Carl's mental banishment:

Carl will find a weak or vulnerable person in the office and begin to complain about his performance.

Carl will break out into sweating at nights.

Carl, resistant to his wife Debra's wish to spend an evening at the home of friends, goes to their house unwillingly and ends up spilling coffee on their carpet.

Carl fantasizes the death of his boss in an air crash.

Carl forgets appointments or details.

Carl complains about the minister at his church because Carl thinks the minister is afraid to speak out on controversial issues.

Carl uses words like "terrific" or "wonderful" or "great"
more frequently even though his back aches increasingly.

Carl banishes his hostility. By ignoring it, Carl "destroys
the evidence." Like blaming, there is an emotional housecleaning, only now swept under the rug rather than thrown
at someone else.

Even if Carl were to describe the percentage of satisfaction
to nonsatisfaction as 100% rather than 80%, whether he is
aware of it or not, the 20% remains. It is simply no longer
available to Carl's consciousness. It is only known by his
unconscious, another mental shed where hurts, unwanted
feelings, or unresolved conflicts are stored. Out of *mind*, out
of *sight*. Carl exchanges choosing to do something about his
discontent for banishing it from his awareness. He does not
complain, remember, mourn, speak out, or search for others. Carl becomes an emotional recluse, obtaining nothing
from the experience nor from others.

Measuring by seeing

When you believe life is unfair, you may deal with it by
throwing your discontent out of proportion to your contentment, either elevating it (brooding) or devaluing it (banishing). Brooding fattens your misery. You permit a smaller
percentage to bear a larger weight. Struggling against the
"unearned unhappiness," you earn some of your own making. On the other hand, when you banish your discontent
you thin its weightiness. You make believe that you are not
troubled by it. You bury it, making it a secret. Again, however, you compound it. Hidden inside, it festers, sneaking
out in ways unknown to you.

Continually whining about his arrogant boss, Carl adds
to his discontent. Or, if Carl continually conceals his frustration, he still expresses it, but unconsciously and indi-
rectly. What change of appraisal would be helpful? I asked

Carl to make a list of ways he could deal with his situation: "If you would do something else, Carl, other than brooding, or possibly banishing, what would you do?" The best suggestions from his list are noted below:

I would tell my boss what I feel—honestly but not judgmentally. I would do this with "I statements," such as "I feel angry when you make decisions that are my responsibility."

I cannot change his personality or behavior. He is who he is—I can only change my feelings and attitudes.

I would appreciate what I have—my children, my wife, the rest of the job, living where I am close to my roots and family.

I would enjoy the other people with whom I work. Instead of giving my boss so much of my energy (emotion, thought, time), and giving it in negative packages, I would give compliments, time, and appreciation to those who I do care about at work.

I would accept my skills and competencies in spite of my boss's need to feel superior by making others, especially me, appear to be inferior.

Life isn't fair. But I am not about to spend a lot of energy complaining about it. Well, yes, I complain. But complain day after day, and in the back room with others—not like before!

Carl's list indicates that he has at his command new ways of seeing and measuring his life. He cannot change the circumstances, but he can proportion his perception more realistically.

Inner attitude

While showing you the new home she is having built, your friend asks if you would mind stopping by the building contractor's office for a few minutes while she takes care of a detail. You consent and drive with her to the builder's office. As she is explaining her question he is tapping his pencil and glancing at the papers scattered on his desk. He answers her with a wave of his hand and turns away to his paperwork. He does not reply as your friend cheerfully thanks him and says good-bye. Taking note of his disregard of your friend, you mention it to her as you leave. She remarks, "He's like that every time I come in." Surprised that she remains undisturbed, you ask how she stays so calm. "Why should I let his behavior," she says, "determine mine?" Your friend chooses the way she wants to *respond* in such circumstances; perhaps you would have *reacted* to what was happening outside yourself.

Julius Lester, who lives in Massachusetts, explains how he deals with long periods of cold weather in his part of the country, being responsive, not reactive ("Dandelion Spring," *Katallagete, Spring 1977*). For six months he accepts the fact that he is going to be cold. When he fights against the cold weather, he finds it more difficult to bear the coldness. The more he resists and complains, the more intolerable the winter climate becomes. Lester keeps the Massachusetts winter in perspective—six months. Instead of allowing the climatic conditions to determine his behavior, he responds. He makes adjustments from within.

Neither your friend nor Julius Lester react by complaining about the external situation. Unlike Carl, who at first lashed out at his supervisor, these two are not looking for fairness, settling scores; they choose not to live underneath their experience. Instead of scorning their circumstance, they adjust their attitude.

What we *want* significantly influences our inner attitude. Our wants are contained in our beliefs, wishes, and expectations. But life is not always fair. Reality has no regard for our wants. There are gaps, rubs, and sore spots; there are unexpected twists and sudden turns. We do not get everything we want. Our wants inevitably collide with the limitations of reality. And how painful it is to trade our perfect wants for imperfect fulfillment. We feel cheated. Brooding over the unfairness, we sink further under the weight of our own frustration. Banishing harsh reality from our awareness, we forfeit our last human freedom—to choose our attitude. We believe we can change reality by merely ignoring it. The last thing we want to change are our own beliefs, wishes, and expectations—ourselves.

To be contented, we do not need complete satisfaction or total justice. We need a new way of seeing life. Our old perceptions are what, in the first place, set up our deep frustrations. "Events give us pain or joy," Paul Tournier writes in *Creative Suffering*, "but our growth is determined by our personal response to both, by our inner attitude." Contentment is in our response, not in our circumstance. How much power we give away to outside reality, whether to an arrogant supervisor, a cranky builder, or cold weather, when we demand that they fit our inner picture. At the same time we have less energy for reappraisal and new choices. We react to the events and live underneath them. Reappraisal only emerges once we cease giving power to past disappointment. Hope is reimagining the future. Life is unfair, but it is not only unfair.

An exercise that can help you use the ideas from this chapter is printed on page 123 in the exercises section.

7

Contentment Is Yours

Your first experience of contentment comes "outside" yourself and as your "right." Entrepreneurs still try to "sell" you contentment, as if you were a child. But contentment becomes less your right and less something outside yourself as you mature. Contentment is now your responsibility.

The first experience

When you are an infant, contentment is mother's breast and, of course, a dry diaper. Within months it is her familiar face and secure embrace. A little later, contentment is a yellow rubber duck and a red plastic rattle, and then a teddy bear or a tattered blanket; later on it is a tricycle, then a bicycle, and eventually a set of keys to your own car; then a college education and travel overseas, followed by a loving spouse, two healthy children who make straight As and are clean from drugs, a fine home with closets lined with goods labeled Gucci and Pucci; then a good job topped with the icing of vacations to Hawaii and Acapulco, being a CEO with "mucho," condo, and limo, and all anchored by a retirement nest of COLAs, CDs, IRAs, and no IOUs.

This picture of contentment is developed from infancy. You learn satisfaction is "out there," full of "things," and whatever you desire will be provided by someone for you. Your parents meet your needs and make your choices. They are intent on pleasing you. You begin to live with the assumption that contentment is your *right*. If it is not provided, you cry or pout to get others to make you happy. Later you add other behaviors: smiling to get your heart's desire, being good to get what you expect. As an infant you are satisfied by something outside yourself—the milk that meets the need of hunger, the hug that satisfies the need of belonging, the blanket that fulfills the need of safety.

During your growing years, a gradual shift occurs. Contentment becomes less your "unalienable right" and more your own responsibility. In the process of growing up, you learn to reduce your reactions (crying, getting angry) and to increase your responses (choosing and risking). Even now your life is an ongoing journey of minimizing reactions and maximizing responses.

Consider my 13-year-old son and my 49-year-old friend. The former wants a bass guitar and guitar lessons. At the moment, however, other items in the family budget must be first. His dilemma is that he is able to delay gratification only for about 30 minutes. He faces a turning point, learning that what he wants is not so much his right but much more his responsibility. So he is saving his money for the purchase of a guitar, discovering along the way that some satisfactions take time before their completion and must come from oneself. Meanwhile my friend, knowing that his cancerous condition would soon have its way, wrote to me during the last months of his life about his discovery. In the process of dying, he recognized his need to be more tolerant both of others and himself. His perception changed. Near death he increased his patience and compassion.

The peddlers of contentment

You carry your childhood picture of reality into adult life. There many messages, especially those of the mass media, arouse your childhood picture. The "hidden persuaders" know how to stir up your early fantasies, to activate your first picture of life (wish plus satisfaction equals reality). The media so often succeed in hooking you by triggering these powerful, primitive pictures. You look outside yourself for the good life; you believe contentment consists of things; you expect to be made happy, or to be stress-free, or to be self-fulfilled. You believe you *find* contentment. It's out there somewhere all wrapped up with your name on it. If you can't find it, you are instructed to try this or that, or you are told that you are not trying hard enough.

Discontented people are today's biggest market. They are prime targets for the contentment pitch. And peddlers appear everywhere, boasting of a secret power to heal life's disappointments or a new technique to eliminate dissatisfaction. They ask you to sell your soul to their magic. The peddlers market contentment as a thing, a product. They capitalize on the widespread belief that contentment is *out there*, not within you. Contentment is some magic, tonic, or heroic. What you need is outside of yourself. You are diverted to change geography or partners, to use a substance or product, to have a new experience or belief. The merchants of merriment apply their tricks and wares to your vulnerability. Like the American Express card, you cannot leave home without their secrets. Magically, they invite you to remain as you are while adding power to you from the *outside*. And yet, by surrendering to their self-assured solutions, you give them power over your life. You deal with your discontent by giving away your responsibility. You chase after rainbows and raptures; you look for the silver lining and the golden touch. In reality, though, you exchange one control (your own appraisal) for another (their promised solution). You allow yourself to be tempted by a "product" before you use your good sense to change your picture. You surrender your last human freedom—to choose a new attitude—while all along it is your best hope.

I received a brochure in the mail announcing a workshop. Participants were promised 200% happiness. Imagine that—not a little or a sweet increase in happiness. No. The promise was a surplus of happiness, more than one person needs. Nonetheless, the workshop sounded enticing. I'm sure that if the happiness I wanted and what I was experiencing were not close to it, I might have grasped at the straw—a "happiness injection."

You will encounter the wonderful wizards who propose that contentment is your birthright, your due reward from others. If contentment is your right, then you can rightfully expect others to meet your "crying needs," or justly manipulate them to satisfy your cravings. "Make me happy!" Of course, this is nothing but your primal expectation, your childhood experience. Then others were responsible for your satisfaction. At that period of life satisfaction did reside outside of yourself. Contentment was "out there" and consisted of "things." But the process of growing up involves a turn of events—you become responsible for yourself. In fact, if you do not change your picture, and seek contentment from within, you remain an eternal suckling. You look for the fountain of life, the holy shrine, or another breast to sustain you. The peddlers prey on your childishness. For the hawkers of happiness in every century deny the reality that contentment is within you. They want to sell it to you.

As you grow up, though, you learn that life is not so absolute. Your own powers are limited. Not every wish of yours comes true. Life itself is not a parent seeking your satisfaction. The "wish as reality" experience is your introduction to life's story. It is not the whole story; it is only one picture from one experience. Indeed it is powerful. But as your craving goes on, satisfaction is broken. Being an adult is learning other parts of the story. You can no longer absolutize the first experience of childhood. Maturity is a discovery—how to relate your longing for happiness with reality. The merchants of merriment sell you a picture of life: you are a consumer of contentment, not a creator of it. They treat you like a child.

New realities

"I'd like to make a motion," TV personality Bob Newhart says, "that we face reality." You wish such and such would happen to escape facing the reality at hand. You live with your old picture in place of risking a new one. You would rather believe life owes you something than to own it for yourself.

I would like to introduce you to people who seconded Newhart's motion. They learned that contentment was their responsibility, not their right. Let's look at what happens when contentment is yours. Megan and Scott, for instance, exemplify married couples who believe their partners owe them satisfaction. Shawn, who is an alcoholic, expects a "thing" to fill his emptiness. And Jackie, wracked by jealousy, wishes her life would be different. All of them discovered the need to change themselves. What they were looking for already resided in themselves.

The acid of disappointment

Megan expected Scott to know what she needed. She was disappointed, almost bitterly. Believing Scott knew what she needed from him, Megan felt hurt when she did not receive it. She kept telling Scott, "You don't care." She reacted by blaming. What was running through Megan's mind was a picture: Scott knows what I need. He won't give it to me, therefore he does not want to give it to me. If he does not want to give it, he does not care about me. Not getting what she wanted, Megan changed her tactics from charm to cruelty. Instead of doing pleasant things, Megan inflicted pain.

Megan placed the entire responsibility for the marital conflict on Scott. Satisfaction is something out there, Megan assumed, that Scott has and knowingly will not give. What Megan was not aware of is that she expected Scott to know what she needed, when, how much, and in what way. Buried deeply in her mental shed stood the old picture—parents who knew her needs and treated them as her rights.

Once Megan took responsibility for her needs, she began to tell Scott what she needed. She recognized her fear that Scott could hurt her in refusing her requests. But she realized that she hurt him in order to avoid feeling hurt herself. As Megan changed her picture of Scott—the all-knowing, always present, and ever-powerful Scott, she changed her feelings and behaviors. In the process Scott changed his picture of Megan—the cruel, spiteful person. Becoming aware of Megan's needs, he could access them more specifically and in a timely way. Intimacy, Scott discovered, is mutual need satisfaction, and the needs are satisfied when the relationship is a "safe place." Scott learned how unsafe their relationship was for Megan when he discounted her. And what was true for Megan was true for Scott. He felt hostile toward Megan when she disregarded his needs.

This couple's power struggle became creative. But it could have been destructive if they had maintained their old pictures of one another, wanting the other to change or coercing the other to change. Again, the acid of disappointment passed because each *responded* to what was hidden, to what was in their own mental shed, and then to what was happening between them.

The deadening of pain

When Shawn's disappointment reached the swelling stage, he reacted with grief. But instead of actually grieving, he "cried in his beer." He handled disappointment with alcohol. I saw Shawn after he had completed a month-long recovery program. Although he was participating in an aftercare support group, Shawn wanted to disclose himself in an arrangement of one-to-one. He gave me the following account of himself:

> I kept telling myself I could handle things. But I went back to the bottle to drown my sorrows. Here I was, feeding myself from a bottle. I never saw my action as nurturing but that's really what it was. I'd become sad, despondent, and then flooded my disappointment with booze. Now I want another kind of nurturing . . . something that comes through people, not beer. I've been living in a world of one. I couldn't trust anyone to care for me, and I wouldn't care for anyone else. So I fed myself with a bottle, like a child feeding itself.

Tucked in Shawn's mental shed were many pictures of abandonment associated with pain. He locked his pain inside to survive the problem of his childhood family which lacked consistency. "You can make it, Shawn, as long as you keep that pain imprisoned." Alcohol became his "jailer," barring pain from his consciousness.

Shawn's new picture of himself emerged from his relationship with Sheila. She gave Shawn permission to be himself, to talk about what was held in secrecy. Shawn had not experienced someone who was as accepting and reliable as Sheila. Shawn had unconsciously looked for people who were not honest, not consistent, and not accepting. Sheila was different. After two years of dating and another two years of marriage, Shawn sought help for his alcoholism. His experience with Sheila influenced and shaped a new image in Shawn's mental shed. Shawn, determined not to give power to the past, to what had happened and could not be changed, changed his own images.

The eyes of envy

Jackie appeared as gracious as she was attractive. She appeared contented in herself and in the expression of herself. Beneath the surface, however, bitterness inflamed her heart. She was even bitter about the bitterness to which she had already given herself. On the anniversary day of her divorce from Stewart she made an appointment with me. "Why can't I forgive him," she sighed, "and get on with my life?"

Stewart had left Jackie for another woman. "She's so plain, so vanilla," Jackie exclaimed. "No one would ever think Stewart would be attracted to her." In a sense Jackie's contentment rested with her beauty. Never before had a male rejected her. Jackie had her way with men. Now she envied the other woman who had what Jackie wanted.

I asked her if she wanted to live the way she was living, bent with jealousy. And I told her that I wondered if she really cared about Stewart but cared mostly about losing him to someone she could not imagine losing him to. She did not readily accept my question. She stopped coming.

Four or five months later, Jackie returned for a visit. She told me that she was seeing another counselor and her life was beginning to change. Nevertheless, she wanted to inform me how important raising the point about jealousy had been for her. She explained:

> I've seldom had cause to be jealous. This feeling was so new, so strong, so overpowering. At first I couldn't identify it. How could I admit it? Then I couldn't let it go. All I wanted was pity, then revenge. I've always been ambivalent about what you called my graciousness and my attractiveness. I really wanted people to like me for me, not for my face. But I relied on my looks. Stewart used to say that I was a Jekyll and Hyde . . . one minute kind and considerate, then the next minute very vain. I didn't accept myself for me. What I was saying, "Accept me," was not what I was doing. My actions said, "Look at me." When Stewart left me, I doubted my beauty, I doubted myself. For once, jealousy entered my life; but it would not let me live. I enjoyed nothing. Until I went to see my aunt, I did not understand what was happening. I couldn't control the feeling of jealousy or get away from it. Somehow I knew without knowing it—that sounds crazy—but I knew in a deeper sense that my aunt was always the one who accepted me as me. After my visit I could see and hear what I could not before.

Like Jackie, if contentment is to be yours, discontent cannot be ignored. During emotional stress, your pain has information. It is not valueless. Our culture has a big stake in shaping you to do something *about* it—wish it away, drink yourself out of it, drug yourself beyond it, consume to diminish it, revenge yourself to rid yourself of it—but not to do something *with* it, such as learn from it.

Pain's information takes time to be recognized. It takes time for a bride to know her husband; it takes time for a child to know who she is; it takes time for the heart to know itself. But the peddlers of contentment whisper, "It takes no time to know anything." For Jackie, it took time to deal with her strange and strong feelings of envy. Knowing is usually not a straight, direct, and quick path.

Meanwhile pain destroys self-acceptance. You unload your burdens not only because they are heavy but also because they throw you off course. Revealing your pain, you want someone to accept you in spite of what's going on within you. It is hard to do it for yourself. Emotional pain is like poison ivy. You are all itch. So Jackie *borrowed* her aunt's acceptance until she could find it again within herself. Healing so often comes from other people's acceptance of you before it comes from within, for the only thing you feel within is rejection. Here, too, the peddlers of contentment deceive you; they ignore the personal touch, the loaning of hope, the stretching of encouragement, the giving of time, the gift of acceptance. In the end, contentment is yours, but along the way, you need people.

An exercise that can help you use in your life the ideas from this chapter is printed on page 124 in the exercises section at the back of the book.

Part Three

Making Changes in Your Life

8

When Discontent Is a Blessing

Disappointment is inevitable, but it is not pathological. It may turn your life toward hopelessness, or it may turn your life around. The difference is in you—how you appraise it, what you learn from it, and how you respond to it.

Two sides of the story

Discontent is useful. It can be as equally creative as destructive. Usually we consider discontent to be harmful:

"What good comes out of all the fussing?"

"Why beat your head against a stone wall?"

"What does complaining ever get you?"

No one goes through life without a few lost dreams, some unfulfilled wishes, and a number of outcomes never attained. Blind alleys. Wild-goose chases. Seeds bearing no fruit. You pass through periods of disenchantment. Relatives seeing your discontent, apply home remedies: "Have a drink!" or "Take two aspirins and a hot shower." Friends offer negative prescriptions: "Don't worry!" or "It's not as bad as you think." Coworkers pour cold water on the flames of your frustration, saying, "Cheer up!" or "Come on, smile." All are well-intentioned. But the folk medicine of relatives, the denial instructions of friends, and the cheerleading of associates minimize what to you is deeply felt dissatisfaction. Instinctively, they react to your discontent as if it is pernicious.

When the shoe of suffering is on someone else's foot, you feel the same awkwardness in the presence of another's discontent. You cover it with a Band Aid of terse advice. You turn the sufferer away from her wounds in favor of your reasons or cheerfulness. "Things have a way of turning out for the best," you say, "and you'll be feeling better in no time." You comfort the discontented with lighthearted solutions.

Whether it is your own restlessness or the uneasiness of others, a defense is set up against the discontent. Your picture of discontent is that of a negative phenomenon, a threat, something without value. Others—as well as yourself—need torn and bleeding people to be well and feeling better. The director of a suicide prevention center reports, for instance, "When the kid comes and says, 'I'm really unhappy, or sad, depressed, my life's a bummer,' the typical parental response is very defensive; they respond by saying, 'Oh, no, everything's fine, don't worry about it, everything will be wonderful!' This starts at a very early age, and communications are cut off." The director notes how the parent neutralizes, even trivializes, the teen's discontent. The parents counteract the discontent with denial. Still, the single most associated factor among suicides is depression.

According to one study, 70% of Americans attribute depression to weakness or a character flaw. This bias continues in spite of the fact that one out of four American women and one out of seven men will suffer from clinical depression during some period of their lives. Obviously depression as a symptom of discontent is quite common, even though it is seen as a personal defect. You usher away the presence of discontent through defensive reactions—acting cheerful, making light of the dissatisfied feelings, or coating the discolored spirit with shiny solutions. You defend against depression by attaching a stigma to it. This is sheer denial, not even good sense. You do this not only with good intentions, but also for the sake of not wanting to deal with your own discomfort in the presence of someone else's. You expect people not to hurt, though all of us do. When you erase the disappointment too early, you take away its stimulation.

Responding to discontent

Discontent is painful. Hence, you bury it, or stigmatize it, or try to exorcize it with pleasant words. You perceive discontent as solely a destructive experience. But consider for a moment the creative side of discontent. It is, for instance, a strong motivation for letting go of old things in order that there might be space for something new. Discontent signals a need for making a change. In fact, change seldom occurs, to any significant degree, apart from the reality of dissatisfaction. So when one can find enough people who dislike the same thing, creators of public opinion can trade on the negative discontent—Mothers Against Drunk Drivers, Weight Watchers, Alcoholics Anonymous, consumer advocates, and human rights movements—to institute change. Some people make use of positive discontent, such as teachers encouraging students who want to improve their grades or a minister inviting hearers to faithfulness—a discontent with the way they are, a longing to become more than they are. Discontent is creative if you are *responsive* to it. For the value of discontent, as with any form of pain, is that it prompts a response. It loses value when you react against it, seeing it merely as a threat to life. When you deny or hide your discontent, refusing to look at yourself, you seal your wound and its poison spreads. Pain, when buried, is expressed in another way, as a symptom.

Pleasure and pain

What lies behind your automatic reactions? Your defensive behaviors? Your hiding of wounds? Your instant solutions? One factor is *how* you regard pleasure and pain. Pleasure affirms life; pleasure energizes. You feel satisfaction when these things happen:

- Life fits together. The pictures in your head agree with what you experience. Expectations and reality meet; the ideal and the real approximate one another.
- Your needs are met. You know what they are. You satisfy them or ask for their satisfaction.
- You feel whole. Self-acceptance is high. Feeling integrated rather than split, you project less and need enemies less often.

Pain is the opposite experience. It denies life; it deprives you of energy. You feel dissatisfied when these things happen:

- Life's reality and your expectations are far apart. Your inner pictures and your experience stand removed from one another. Expectation is betrayed by reality.
- Your needs "go crying." You feel unfulfilled and empty.
- You feel split and divided, not at one with yourself. Discontented with yourself, you complain about others.

As long as you experience pleasure, you seek to continue it, even to expand it. But pain cripples. You want it to cease, or at least to diminish in its severity. So quite naturally you maximize your pleasure and minimize your pain. Pleasure signifies life, but pain equals death. You carry the following mental equations:

Pleasure = Life	Pain = Death
Pleasure = Affirmation	Pain = Destruction
Pleasure = Bonding	Pain = Dividing
Pleasure = Continuation	Pain = Cessation

Growing pains

You can *grow* through pain; you grow in a situation that frustrates you. If you do not rub against something or someone, you cannot grow. Your frustration forces you to come to terms with the split between the ideal and the real, the needs that go unattended, and the feelings of self-alienation. Pain teaches. Much of what you learn happens with rubbings, frictions, and tensions—whether it is learning to ride a bike, to speak in public, or to relate with people. Pain is a strong motivating force for change. I do not want to glamorize pain; that is, to set it up as something you look for or welcome. Pain can be either danger or opportunity. As opportunity, it can be a "germinating darkness."

If you had breakfast this morning of eggs, bacon, and toast, you have energy and life because a chicken did not hatch, a pig lost its life, and living wheat germs were crushed. We live because an animal or a plant, some living organism, has died. If you jogged this morning, following the two miles with fifty sit-ups, you are a living testimony to the proverbs of physical conditioning—"No pain, no gain" or "If it hurts, it helps." Even if you missed breakfast and shunned early morning exercise, you nevertheless underwent a growing experience, a death and a resurrection. After 6–10 hours of sleep and a loss of consciousness, you have awakened with renewed energy and a fresh perspective on a new day.

What is true physically is likewise true psychologically. A major disappointment or an emotional hurt can reduce your confidence and gnaw away at your sense of self-worth. Without any conscious effort on your part, your psyche goes to work to bring some degree of equilibrium to your life. You *rationalize* what happened, believing that a pain with reason is better than a senseless one. Or you *compensate* for the pain by sleeping longer, going shopping, or watching a movie.

Growing pains are central to the spiritual life as well. Jesus speaks of the seed that must die before it can bear fruit; he speaks of the person who finds life in losing it. Unless one is willing to shed the adult character armor, Jesus announces, the thickened walls of defenses, the adult roles and masks, one cannot enjoy the presence of God.

The opportunity to create

Discontent in itself is not creative, but it is an opportunity for a creative response. When the pain of discontent is profound, you enter a shadowy world, a dark tunnel. But sometimes when it is dark, you are set free. Going through a long or painful process causes you to let go of something, to learn to live again. At first, though, you are overwhelmed. Gradually you begin to get some sense of reality, some new perspective, some clarity, a different understanding of how you can deal with things as they are.

No matter what disappointment is in you, whether grief over the loss of a loved one, confusion about an image of yourself, worry over career and money, or frustration at the crumbling of a vision, you are thrust into the role of being a *creator*. Discontent makes an artist of you no matter what dream has not come true, what need has been starved or neglected, what thing about yourself you have tried to forget. You are called upon to paint new scenarios out of old scenes, to weave fresh designs out of yesterday's fabric, and to sculpt different forms from the broken pieces. You no longer live according to your old beliefs, wishes, or expectations. You see life as it really is. You are forced to deal with the distance between the fantasy of Cloud 9 and the reality of 10 Main Street. You go through a suffering stage until it succeeds in reshaping your life. If discontent does not push and pull and tug and wrench and twist—and hurt—you are not creatively responding to it; discontent is deadly if it does not move and drive.

The invincible

Rick is a strong, stoic person, but a heart attack at 47, in more ways than one, "laid him low." He assured his family that he would be back on his feet in a few weeks. Rick resented the hospital protocol—the monitoring, the medicating, the utter dependency of it all. One day he told the nurse, "Look, I'm as good as gold. Stop fussing with me. Leave me alone." She calmly responded, "If you had not received help here, you would have been as good as dead."

Three months after his hospital stay, Rick came to see me. His work schedule was limited. Much to his chagrin, the road to recovery was long and tedious. "I'm not," he declared, "the person I used to be." In spite of Rick's exterior bravado, he was sometimes depressed and did not feel like doing anything. "This is not at all like me," he reported, "I thought I would bounce right back."

Overwhelmed at first, Rick began to take his experience with a dosage of honesty and realize he was not invincible.

Rick discovered an appreciation for little things. He noted one day, "This morning I sat on the deck with a cup of coffee and listened to the birds, looked at the cloud formations, and even felt the breeze." Rick's misfortune became creative because he *responded* to it.

Becoming aware

After the crash of a commercial airliner in which most of the passengers died, a survivor learned something afresh. Before the crash, the survivor said he had disregarded the requests of his three-year-old son by saying, "Wait a minute." Now, the man emphasized, he pays immediate attention to his son, for there may not be a tomorrow. Crisis became opportunity, but only because the survivor responded to it. Like most of us, the man lived by habit and did things automatically. He did not give a second thought to the disregard of his son's requests. But surviving a fiery crash jarred him into a new awareness of the uncertainties of life and brought a fresh responsiveness to his son's needs.

You are a creature of habit; you take things for granted. You cannot be aware of everything. By putting your life on "automatic pilot" you don't have to worry about as much. If you had to be aware of and think about every little thing you would be overwhelmed. You need a certain degree of habit in order to survive. But beyond a certain degree, blocked-out awareness has negative consequences. You would not have a choice to make changes because you would not know what you were doing. W. H. Auden writes in *The Age of Anxiety* (Edward Mendelson, ed., Random House, Inc., 1947):

We would rather be ruined than changed,
We would rather die in our dread

> Than climb the cross of the moment
> And let our illusion die.

Discontent, especially if it is strong or prolonged, may be neglected or numbed. But both the intensity and the duration of your discontent show that you need to pay attention to what it is trying to say. It has important information for you.

A sudden loss or a near disaster jolts you. Your feelings of discontent and bodily discomfort carry information; information that your mind usually tries to reject. The mind, functioning as a *reducing valve*, shuts out what is unexpected or painful. At those times, your feelings and body become avenues for information shut out from your mind—to put you on alert, to get a point across, to get the news out.

Choosing to change

Information is only information; it alone is not enough. Knowing something is painful does not mean you will choose to change. Sheldon Kopp writes in *If You Meet the Buddha on the Road Kill Him!* (Toronto-New York-London: Bantam Books, 1972):

> And so, it is not astonishing that, though the patient enters therapy insisting that he wants to change, more often than not, what he really wants is to remain the same and to get the therapist to make him feel better. His goal is to become a more effective neurotic, so that he may have what he wants without risking getting into anything new. He prefers the security of known misery to the misery of unfamiliar insecurity.

"Known misery" feels safer than changing. How you would rather choose to "be ruined than changed," to suffer needlessly rather than do what you need to do to go through it and remove it.

People who need people

Sometimes a jarring experience alone is enough motivation for change. Then you act as your own teacher. At other times change is not easy. You need a teacher along the way. You need a friend who sees more than you see, who helps you find what is real. Because all you can think of is your problem, you need a guide who asks questions to get you to see things in a new way, to challenge your tunnel vision of false beliefs.

If your guide is a compulsive healer, giving you answers but not asking you questions, he or she will not give you any lasting help. A genuine guide does not "solve" your problems or "explain" your miseries, but helps you to be aware of them and identify them. A teacher who has all the answers for you may comfort you but does not challenge you to face the pain courageously and move toward healing.

You need a teacher who encourages you. For it takes courage to tolerate painful awareness. Courage is contagious—we draw it from one another. If hope is a virtue in a hopeless situation, if faith is a power when you cannot see, if love is deepest when the loveless are its object, then courage is real only when something needs to be overcome. Courage is not something you stack in quantity on the shelf of the soul's closet. "Courage mounteth with occasion" wrote Shakespeare in *King Lear*. A guide assists you in drawing out *your* courage. So the more you use courage, the more you have it. Thus you need a guide who will not accept your helplessness. Moreover, you need a guide who will not make choices for you, rendering you even more helpless. A true friend always calls you to your own power, to take responsibility for yourself, to see things in a new way.

You need a wise friend who permits you to be discontented, who knows that tension sharpens your senses and increases your awareness. A good teacher knows that the source of discontent is within you, that pictures you have forgotten are stored in your mental shed and affect the way you feel.

You need a guide who helps you imagine what you cannot imagine by yourself, who helps you face what you believe you cannot face. When a guide sees you as endowed with creativity, and prods it from you, he or she is an artist helping you to be one too. Such a guide who knows that discontent has within itself the seed of recovery leads you to a health found by courage.

The deeper courage

Your helplessness is only the first sign of discouragement. A second symptom is hopelessness, perhaps accompanied by bitterness or dissatisfaction. A guide who provokes your attention will prod your responsiveness and encourage you to begin again. Breaking into your grief or discontent, a guide moves you beyond the powerlessness of the moment. Nonetheless, neither the most responsive person nor the most skilled counselor can remove all the bits and pieces of life's limitations.

As you will see in the next chapter, Christians accept the limitations of human experience. And yet, even though conditions are unfavorable and circumstances seem to deny hope, they trust God to make interventions into their discouragement. They trust that God has broken the chain of sin and death through Jesus Christ; they trust the Holy Spirit's intervention in their behalf with "sighs too deep for words" because they do not know how to pray as they ought. Christians trust God's leading to greater strength through discontent, even when swollen to the point of despair. God's promises are directed precisely to human limitations; God will not break the crushed reed or quench the wavering flame or despise a broken and contrite heart. Faith, a deeper kind of courage, believes God's power is made perfect in human weakness: your limitations, your discouragement, your discontent.

That faith helps you realize how much God loves you. That faith is the deeper kind of courage that asks for guidance and strength each step of the way. God's answers to your prayers may take many forms: human beings who love you and care what happens, worship experiences with others, feelings of reassurance (rare at first but more common as you continue to ask), events, experiences, or a book or Bible reading that speaks to your heart. God is always with you and God's love for you is unwavering.

An exercise that can help you use in your life the ideas from this chapter is printed on page 125 in the exercises section.

9

The Restless Heart

Discontent is a major theme in the Bible. The apostle Paul, who suffers much, reveals that he learned how to be content by, of all things, being weak. He learned to trust God's grace in Jesus Christ.

Agitation and grievance

Plenty of discontent is recorded in the Bible. It reads life with realism. In the Old Testament, for instance, Cain's envy of Abel erupts into murder. The jealous brothers of Joseph sell him to traders. Wandering in the desert, the Israelites complain to Moses that "we never see anything but this manna." They hanker for the days in Egypt where their appetites were sated with cucumbers, melons, leeks, onions, and garlic. Exasperated, Moses complains to God about "the burden of all these people." Later, King Hezekiah, to whom God promises 15 years of royalty, is dissatisfied with the terms and arranges a political pact to fortify his rule. Job complains that his eyes "have grown dim with grief." An entire writing is called "Lamentations." Even the great devotional book of Israel, the Psalms, carries constant cries of discontent:

O my God, I cry out by day, but you do not answer, by night, and am not silent.   (Ps. 22:2)

As the deer pants for streams of water, so my soul pants for you, O God. My soul thirsts for God, for the living God. When can I go and meet with God? . . . Why are you downcast, O my soul? Why so disturbed within me?
(Ps. 42:1-2,11)

The same realism is reflected in the New Testament. The Pharisees murmur against Jesus because he "receives sinners and eats with them." When a village of Samaritans rejects Jesus, James and John want to consume the village with fire. And when James and John request seats of honor in the kingdom of God, the other disciples grumble against them. The bold disciple, Peter, weeps bitterly when his boldness gives way to a cowardly denial of knowing Jesus.

Learning the secret

If any New Testament figure had a reason to complain, it certainly was the apostle Paul. As a persecutor of the Christians, the community was suspicious of him when he became a part of it. As an apostle of Jesus Christ, he reached the point of being "under great pressure, far beyond [his] ability to endure" that he despaired of life itself. He reports that he was whipped five times, beaten with rods three times, and stoned once; shipwrecked, he was adrift at sea. Paul faced the dangers of rivers and robbers, hunger and thirst, cold and exposure. Due to his poor physical appearance and speaking ability, his opponents mocked his preaching of the gospel, the good news of Jesus Christ, and questioned its importance. So Paul describes himself as "one abnormally born" and "the least of the apostles."

Nevertheless, Paul could exclaim that "in all things God works for the good of those who love him." He was convinced that nothing could separate him from the love of God revealed in Jesus Christ. "We are hard-pressed on every side," he writes, "but not crushed; perplexed, but not in despair; persecuted, but not abandoned; struck down, but not destroyed" (2 Cor. 4:8-9). Out of his own troubling experiences came the picture of a gracious God—"I have learned to be content whatever the circumstances. I know what it is to be in need, and I know what it is to have plenty. I have learned the secret of being content in any and every situation, whether well fed or hungry, whether living in plenty or in want. I can do everything through him who gives me strength" (Phil. 4:11-13). Paul learned contentment, not by skirting around discontent, but by going *through* all sorts of disappointments, limitations, and a wide range of human emotions.

One of Paul's greatest interpreters, Martin Luther, expresses how he too learned of a gracious God by living, by dying, by being damned, by going where his temptations took him. Neither Paul's nor Luther's experience was caused by the gracious God; their experience was the opportunity for learning. The gracious God was always there but only became real to them in their restlessness, in their discontent. Both men were drawn, pushed, and dumped into learning how to be content. The love of God expressed in Jesus Christ gave them a vantage point to combat the limitations and disappointments of life. Paul, for example, makes no claim that he overcame reality. God did not change reality for Paul's convenience. God's love changed Paul. In Paul's mental shed stood the image of Jesus Christ, "one who has been tempted in every way, just as we are," one who is "merciful and faithful," one who "is able to deal gently with those who are ignorant and are going astray, since he himself is subject to weakness," one who is able "to sympathize with our weaknesses," and one who tasted "death for every one."

Paul draws his strength from Christ. No matter what the circumstances may be, before and after, above and below, beyond and within all reality, there is a Gracious One. Nothing comes your way that has not passed through the hands of Christ. Looking upon your bitter disappointments with love and compassion, Christ offers the comfort and the courage to endure because he has been there.

The candy machine god

Shirley Guthrie ("The Narcissism of American Piety: The Disease and the Cure," *Journal of Pastoral Care*, vol. 31, no. 4, Dec. 1977, pp. 222-223) characterizes a group of discontented people by the way they believe in God. "God is the candy machine," Guthrie notes, "whose purpose is to meet our needs, solve our problems, answer our questions, give us whatever we happen to want most." The great heavenly candy machine is the dispenser of goodies—the doting heavenly grandparent, the administrator of celestial welfare programs, the unseen errand boy who runs and gets what the people want. Like children, this group demands that the candy machine God grant their longings immediately, even lavishly. They *believe* the "good news" of the Bible is a "good deal" for themselves. God is useful. They *wish* God would change reality so they don't have to change their own attitudes. These people *expect* God to perform miracles for their convenience. Everything is direct and quick, like the magical world of the small child.

The same group could be said to compare God to a gigantic aspirin. Aching from their disappointments, they want God to relieve them of the pain of reality. If God cannot make them feel better, then God is unnecessary. In the words of one of William Faulkner's characters: "It's got to be honeymoon, always" (from *Honeymoon All the Time*). There will be no "terrible disappointment in love" for them.

Out of their groping discontent, people imagine a candy-machine God or a gigantic aspirin. But what kind of a God is this? Certainly it is not a God to be feared, loved, and trusted above all things, in any and all circumstances. Rather, it is a God who is believed because you get the things you want. Yet how can you trust a God whom you can control? A candy machine God, nickled and dimed, is at your mercy, at your disposal. How can you stand in awe of a God who exists only for the sake of your momentary advantage? It is a God defined solely by your own longing. It is an image based on the experience of childhood, when wishes were fulfilled and pleasures were frequent. It is not a God who defines himself by his longing for his people, before and apart from any human yearning.

The candy-machine God is not the God Paul encountered in both the bitter and sweet experiences of life. For Paul, the gracious God is one who longs for what he created. He sums up God's longing in the word *grace*. Grace is a free gift. It is given without regard for a return; it is given without regard for any demand. Grace is God's acceptance of you prior to and independent of any longing you have, any action you take, any circumstance you experience. Grace means God is *for* you. God *first* loves you. Before you are aware of your own groping discontent, God is already longing for you, longing for you so deeply that God gave his one and only Son in your behalf. "But God demonstrates his own love for us in this," Paul states. "While we were still sinners, Christ died for us" (Rom. 5:8).

Empowerment

How God searches for those he longs for tells you worlds about God. He reveals who he is in "Christ crucified." God makes himself known in love and suffering, in darkness and silence, in disappointment and discontent. Paul rejects the candy machine God who is based on childish wishes and groping discontent. Speaking of his own experience, Paul writes:

> When I was a child, I talked like a child, I thought like a child, I reasoned like a child. When I became a man, I put childish ways behind me. Now we see but a poor reflection as in a mirror; then we shall see face to face. Now I know in part; then I shall know fully, even as I am fully known.
> (1 Cor. 13:11-12)

The child thinks everything should be perfect. "Childish ways" demand all of it, all of it now, and all of it now "only for me." But the mark of maturity is to accept what is partial, what is not fully understood, what appears dim. Paul learned that he could not demand a perfect fit between reality and his beliefs, wishes, and expectations. What gave Paul strength in any and all circumstances was the knowledge that God fully understood him. God knows the "heartaches and thousand natural shocks" of reality firsthand. God was in "Christ crucified."

Centuries before Paul, the prophet Isaiah spoke to the groping discontent of the people of Israel, pointing to the gracious promise of God:

> He gives strength to the weary and increases the power of the weak. Those whose hope is in the Lord will renew their strength. They will soar on wings like eagles; they will run and not grow weary, they will walk and not be faint (Isaiah 40:29, 31).

Isaiah does not speak of solutions and satisfactions. He speaks about *empowerment*. Those who hope in the Lord receive increased and renewed *strength*. Paul, likewise, receives no direct and immediate satisfaction to his longings. He learned from the Lord "My grace is sufficient for you, for my power is made perfect in weakness" (2 Cor. 12:9). Paul became aware of God's empowerment through his own weakness. He had a new picture in his mental shed; no solutions but strength; no explanations but assurance; no direct results but a gradual encouragement; no daily newscasts from Celestial Communications but a promise; no fast and straight gratification but the Holy Spirit as the guarantee of God's presence; no full understanding but a faithful God who understands. So when reality missed or contradicted Paul's beliefs, wishes, or expectations, he learned to live in the middle of reality. He did not live underneath his experience in despair or above it in "solutions." God's grace became the support Paul trusted in any and all circumstances.

Paul *learned* how to be content. He experienced no instant victories. Learning always takes time. If you insist on immediate satisfactions, you simply betray your own restless heart—how overwhelmed and threatened you feel. For the circumstance of discontent throws you back to the most primitive experience, the experience of the small child's "terrible disappointment in love," an image stored in your mental shed. No wonder, therefore, that Paul urges, "Stop thinking like children. . . . In your thinking be adults" (1 Cor. 14:20). He prods you to go beyond the picture based on childhood experience. As a child you were used to "comfort-health"—the picture of well-being when things go your way and you get what you want. But as an adult you need to learn the significance of "courage-health"—the picture of going on with life in spite of your restless, unfulfilled longings. This is precisely Paul's picture. God longs for you; God is always there first. He will empower you to respond, not pamper you in your reactions.

The velvet wand

When Heather came to see me, she was determined to receive relief from her pain. She believed I would meet her needs, solve her problems, and give her what she wanted most—the end of her suffering. At the time, however, Heather did not understand that therapy is a matter of pain itself. She wanted instant service. But therapy calls for courage in recognition of the pictures in the mental shed and all the pain associated with them. With time Heather gave up her demand for comfort and began to draw on courage. At the end of our time together, she presented me with a gift— a velvet wand she made with the stitched inscription, *This does not work*. Heather thought it might be useful as a visual aid, especially for others who, like herself, wanted relief without change, magic instead of reality, solutions rather than picking out the briars one by one where she was.

It is foolish to insist that discontent is unnecessary. The question is not really how you keep from being disappointed. Discontent comes in spots and spurts. The essential question is What are you going to do with your discontent? What is helpful in going *through* it to the other side? What has the capacity to breed hope? To what power do you give yourself to deal with your disappointments?

A candy-machine God, a velvet-wand therapist, whatever, these were not the means behind Paul's learning to be content in all circumstances. Living among the briars, Paul relates how he sought three times to have God remove his thorny discontent. Even as Jesus prayed that "the cup" be removed, so also Paul prayed that his "thorn" be removed.

Paul used up his nickels and dimes. Paul discovered that the candy machine was busted, actually it never existed at all. He learned that pain is the home of courage, that human weakness is a sacred place, that what he suffered now would be revealed later as the circumstance in which God's grace was sufficient. Thus Paul fit the passing moment into a larger time span, something a child cannot do. Being "fully persuaded that God had power to do what he had promised" (Rom. 4:21), Paul pictured life as accommodating any disappointment without having its light overshadowed by disappointment. Unlike the candy-machine-God proponents, Paul did not reward discontented people for their childishness through instant solutions. Instead, he directed people to trust God above all things by *waiting*.

Waiting for the promise

Patience? Conventional wisdom teaches that "haste makes waste" and "patience is a virtue." But then it suggests that "he who hesitates is lost" and "the sleeping fox catches no poultry." So you live between "all good things come to those who wait" and "the early bird gets the worm." You live with two images.

Today's world is fast-paced, bent on saving time, and geared to direct results. It favors the early bird over the sleeping fox. Though satellites and electronic discs provide up-to-the-minute information and instant replay, people themselves cannot be "speeded up." People change slowly and gradually, sometimes begrudgingly. Human beings are part of nature with its seasons and cycles and rhythms. Living with the forceful images of speed and results, you can hardly picture waiting as anything but feeble. But much of the bitter disappointment you experience comes from the picture of getting what you want—here and now. You cram eternity into a lifetime. God is too slow. You want to run ahead of him. You want your beliefs to match the moment; you want to catch up with your wishes; you want to overtake your expectations. In the fury of haste you set yourself up for deeper disappointment. Going through experiences as fast as you do, you have no time to gather together the stones of courage, to hold an event long enough in your attention to probe beneath the surface, to stretch your imagination and pull life together.

Paul's "secret" of being content in any and all circumstances is based on waiting. It is the primary characteristic of faith in the Bible. Paul learned that discontent is not subject to quick relief. Therefore he does not picture faith as an overnight cure or a way to get rapid results. Faith neither protects you against discontent nor pulls you from the realities of life. Instead faith is an *imaginative power*. Not all the facts and possibilities are in yet; not all the mysteries and promises have yet played their hand.

The pictures in your mental shed, formed through your experiences, represent the way you experience the world. And they are the instruments you use to manage your world. Nonetheless, they are not the only pictures of life. In fact, a major consequence of discontent is the loss of imaginative power. You only draw upon one set of pictures, those confirming your disappointment. You are preoccupied. The mental shed is closed. You cannot imagine anything else. But Paul urged that there be a transformation by the renewal of the mind, by another set of pictures—"to know the mind of God with which to see [the love of Christ] that surpasses knowledge" (Eph. 3:19). God fulfills his longing for you in the love of Christ, so that you may be awakened to his *faithfulness* to you. But how will you know his faithfulness if you do not know his silence and absence? How can children learn to trust their mother apart from her going away and returning?

One of the most difficult disciplines of the spirit is to "be still," to remain at the point of need, to stand persistently, if not stubbornly, where restlessness is most intense—and still not to be tempted, enticed, or distracted away by easy magic or instant solution. This is the hardest thing to learn—how to be disappointed, to know you are disappointed, to bear patiently the burden of disappointment and not reach for illusion, the glow of elsewhere, or the peddler's pitch; and not to withdraw into your darkness, going underneath your experience. To wait until God returns is painful, but patience is not deadly. To wait is to deal with hopelessness, and not panic like a child at any and every twinge of disappointment. Faith is the imaginative power to act even though circumstances are overwhelming and conditions are unfavorable. The promise of God is that he will not remain silent. He will fulfill his own longing for you. Only he sets the speed, shapes the satisfaction, and determines the place. God is oblivious to the job descriptions people write for him. God will not permit himself to be used by those who want something from him. But God does not envy you your happiness; he insists that it be on his terms—his own steadfast love for you.

An exercise that can help you use in your life the ideas from this chapter is printed on page 126 in the exercises section.

10

Stepping into the Picture

The most significant changes in your mental pictures and movement toward contentment occur under three conditions—a safe place, a new experience, and an emotional struggle.

Where is Brooklyn?

A scholarly art professor talked about visiting Europe to view all the masterpieces. He never made the visit. The professor said lack of money was the primary reason. When he received a grant to visit the museums of Europe, he passed it over and stayed at home. Perplexed, he sought counseling. There he discovered that his resistance was deeply embedded: "My father never left Brooklyn."

You will have your "Brooklyns," wedded to familiar faces and adjusted to safe places. The psyche knows the crisis of separation—whether it is loss, change, or the unexpected. Your mental shed, full of images, makes your world familiar and safe. Like the professor, you may not be aware of the images held in storage. Even if you become aware, and a certain picture is contradicted by events, the old picture stubbornly prevails. A team loses a playoff game, for instance, and yet it believes it is the better of the two opponents. A mother's picture of her son, dented and crushed by his criminal behavior, remains unchanged. "He's a good boy," she protests. "That's not like him. They have the wrong person." Or a noted personality is exposed as a deceiver, a sham; nevertheless, admirers and followers blame others, not her.

Even if you become aware, and the picture is something you want to change, there is no assurance that you will. Addicted, a woman claims, "I'll quit tomorrow." But she doesn't. Feeling guilty about the neglect of his children, a father resolutely announces, "I'll spend more time at home." But he doesn't. Embroiled in a bitter power struggle, a couple agrees to behave differently. Still, he abuses her physically, and she alternately attacks him with words and herself with blame. All of them are stuck in their own version of "Brooklyn." Can a career-minded woman will to be a traditional housekeeper? Can a couple will to be intimate? Human beings have an immense capacity for resisting change, even when they are wise and well-meaning. The "can do" spirit is exciting. But it neglects the strength of your mindset. Your mental pictures make your world seem simple, familiar, and secure. Better the security of your "known misery," as Sheldon Kopp says, than the misery of "unknown insecurity"—will or no will. "My father never left Brooklyn."

Three conditions

Change is most likely under three conditions: (1) being at ease in a safe place, where openness is encouraged, (2) participating in a new experience, responding in a different way, (3) struggling with emotional tension, approaching despair. Your attention is excited; your awareness is sharpened. New pictures, like old pictures already stored, begin with an experience—you are moved. There is a readiness. Memories are set free. Visions are stretched.

The three people discussed below illustrate how one of the three conditions prepared them for stepping into their pictures, for rummaging around in their mental shed, and eventually for the discovery of a renewed sense of being "at one" and once again saying yes to life.

A safe place

Paul is a 37-year-old minister. He is intelligent and outgoing. A recent seminary graduate, Paul's first assignment was to a small congregation in a historic southern town. Two weeks after Paul's arrival, his mother died in California. When he returned from the funeral, he learned that the congregation was rekindling an old internal conflict, one Paul had been assured was a thing of the past. The people were not emotionally available to the grieving pastor. Moreover, Paul's wife, unable to find employment as a dental assistant, was feeling useless and isolated. She reported her conversation with a physician in town to her husband. "Don't expect people to become your friends," he mentioned, "You are born here, and you die here."

Over the next several months, her loneliness intensified. While she felt miserable, one of their sons, a second-grader, kept waking up crying in the middle of the night; but he was unable to answer his parents' questions about what was wrong. Later they learned that some children in school were taunting him, saying his father believed in Satan. Paul himself was overeating, not sleeping, on the edge at work, not

knowing what people wanted him to do about their skir-
mishing. Finally he visited a physician, complaining of
headaches and dizziness. Medication relieved Paul's physical pain, but the lack of motivation remained. In his mind
he kept tossing a comment from his physician that if Paul
had "more faith" he would not feel as he did. Confused and
deflated, he visited a local mental health clinic, but only
once. The counselor's first words mocked ministers in general: "You ministers have so much trouble." On his way
home he stopped at another minister's home, looking for
help. This, too, proved futile. The minister could not em-
pathize with Paul because he denied ever feeling down. Furthermore, he spent most of their time together talking about
his church's new organ.

When Paul came to see me, he was at the brink of tears.
"I can't believe what's happened in only six months," he
lamented, "I've never experienced anything like this before.
I don't care anymore." Paul's grief, grounded in reality,
kept coming to the surface in our early visits. Then one day
he remembered his pain from the past:

> When I was 17, my girlfriend broke up with me. I wouldn't
> talk to anyone. I moped around. Felt so empty. Really, I
> don't know how I survived those months. Everyone told me
> to forget her. Get on with life. But I couldn't . . . or wouldn't.
> I never wanted to feel that way again. Never! And here I am
> with the same feelings building up in me. . . .

Stored in Paul's mental shed stood the picture of the wound-
ed lover. Aware of the old picture, Paul admitted to his fear
of grieving now, like then, with prolonged intensity.

I will never forget Paul. He taught me a lesson. "You are
the only one," he observed, "who has let me have my pain."
Paul was telling me that he felt *safe*. No cures. No advice.

No explanations. Being in a safe place, he was able to retrieve from rusted memory the old picture of pain. He became aware of "Brooklyn" and feared it.

Learning happens when people feel safe to express how they really feel. For if learning environments are threatening, painful pictures can neither be exposed nor expressed. And if you cannot see them, how can you step into the pictures and change them? Learning occurs in a reliable, relaxed setting, where you are tended to just as you are. In fact, the word *school* is derived from the Greek word meaning "leisure time." Nowhere is the sense of ease and safety required more than when you deal with mental pictures associated with pain, like Paul's grief and fear.

This is clearly depicted in the Bible, when Jesus, seeing the crowds "harrassed and helpless," takes compassion on them and begins to teach them. On another occasion Jesus extended the invitation, "Come to me, all you who are weary and burdened, and I will give you rest. Take my yoke upon you and learn from me, for I am gentle and humble in heart" (Matt. 11:28-29). Jesus did not rush them into *cure;* he first expressed *care.* Neither did he deny their weariness or burdens. Instead he offered rest and a gentle and humble heart—a safe place where they could learn. Jesus sets them at ease, releasing them from the cramped dimension of their images and feelings of the moment.

A new experience

How could "the little boy" fill "a man's shoes?" That was Jason's question. Apparently the 36-year-old educator had everything going for him. Both competent and friendly, Jason received an appointment to a position of leadership. Nevertheless he felt discontented. Rather than liking his advanced status, he disliked it. Unknown to others, Jason's

image of himself included "the little boy," one less significant than others. He grew up as the youngest of three sons
and deferred to his older brothers. As a teenager he grew
more slowly than most his age. "I can't hide in my room
anymore," Jason mused; "now I have to give speeches, evaluate others, and make policy decisions." How was "the little
boy" ever going to be at ease at work? How could Jason
experience himself in a different way? What behaviors could
be changed in order to change his picture of himself?

In order to develop a more confident, mature image of
himself, Jason outlined specific ways of behaving he wanted
to change. By experiencing himself differently, Jason set
out to step into his picture. To expand his awareness of the
ways he wanted to act, I suggested that he carry a pack of
ten toothpicks wrapped in a rubber band. He was to put
them in his pocket, even to shower and sleep with them.
Whenever he acted on one of the chosen behaviors, he would
remove one toothpick. If he reverted to the old experience
of the little boy, he would add a toothpick. Then, at each
session, Jason would count the toothpicks and review the
behaviors. Every time we met, Jason practiced one of the
new ways of behaving with me. Through these simulations
he experienced himself in a different way. Simply, you cannot do it without *doing* it. If new behaviors are not repeated,
you slide back to the old ones. The old pictures triumph.

Jason learned that the mental picture of the little boy was
a longstanding consequence of *disowning* his own anger.
Whatever you do not take responsibility for is passed onto
others. You pass on not only your unwanted, negative side
of yourself, as in the psychological bath (Chapter 5), but
also positive, powerful parts of yourself. By lowering his
own significance, Jason gave greater significance to others.
In childhood he passed it onto his brothers; in adolescence
he projected it onto his peers. Now, as the leader himself,

there was no place to project it. He had to learn to take responsibility for it himself.

Jason learned that he did not have to reject the old picture of the little boy in order to be a more confident, mature person. The old picture was the source of his friendliness, so attractive to others. A new picture gained through a new experience allows you to be more than what you pictured before. Jason imagined himself as both the little boy and the respected leader.

Once again the Bible depicts one of the conditions of learning—stepping into your picture through a new experience. Jesus remarks that "unless you change and become like little children," "unless he is born again," "unless your righteousness surpasses that of the Pharisees and teachers of the law," "unless a kernel of wheat falls to the ground and dies, it remains only a single seed. But if it dies, it produces many seeds." Jesus says there must be a change in one's way of thinking, one's attitude, one's outlook. The pictures you form from your experiences are limited, partial. There is more to life than the pictures in your mental shed. If God's "thoughts are not your thoughts," there needs to be *repentance*, which means "a change of mind." Repentance is moving from "Brooklyn" (your own experience) to "Bethlehem" (God's experience of taking on human flesh and offering grace), thereby experiencing yourself anew.

Emotional struggle

Sometimes reality comes as a shock. It is heavy. It has dark corners and sharp edges. At first, wanting pleasure, you resist the pain. You try to change the world or other people, not yourself. You react to what is outside of you instead of responding to yourself:

You deny reality;

You pretend all is well;

You tranquilize or dull your pain;
You trivialize the events;
You accuse others;
You look for a quick cure;
You believe in magic;
You fall into helplessness;
You curse your lot in life.

Reactions, however, hinder self-reflection: "What's happening? What do I feel? What did I expect? What can I do?" Only as your reactions diminish can you become aware of yourself and make a new appraisal.

Consider Allison. She is a well-known, well-liked woman of 42. Taking part in many groups and activities, Allison has a wide range of acquaintances and friends. None of them would have guessed that hidden in Allison's mental shed stood a picture of her as the lonely one. Her frantic pace had simply covered it over from her and others' view. The picture developed in her family experiences, a mother who used emotional rejection to manipulate her and a father who imprisoned his emotions from her. Allison's picture of the lonely one was caused emotionally.

She came to see me, believing her husband was going to leave her. Not known to Allison, she dealt with her hidden inner picture by binding people to herself and making them dependent on her. What she did not realize was that the binding of others to herself kept her bound to them as well. Her husband's threats of leaving terrified her. The reality was shocking. Allison's discontent took the form of overeating. Unconsciously, she was affirming her picture of the lonely one: "See, you are unattractive; you will be abandoned." Trying to counteract her husband's threat, she acted in the way she knew best—binding him to her, always trying hard to please him. "For heaven's sake," he shouted, "can't you leave anyone alone. Go lose some weight!"

She thought: "If I get close emotionally, he'll abandon me." He thought: "If I get close emotionally, she'll suffocate me." Consequently, Allison would risk closeness only by doing things. Meanwhile her husband, Bart, would risk closeness only by first distancing himself. While both Allison and Bart had pictures in need of change, we will stay with Allison's for the sake of illustration. As long as she maintained her picture of the lonely one, she would self-fulfill the picture. "What determines one's being," Abraham Heschel remarks in *Who Is Man?*, "is the image one adopts." First, of course, Allison had to *see* the image, covered as it was by her endless activities. Once she recognized the image and the experience out of which it was spun, she could choose to balance it with another picture.

Allison discovered another image already in her mental shed. She told me the story of a summer vacation with her grandparents full of delight and pleasure. Her grandfather read her books; her grandmother helped her make jellies and jams. Among her stored images was one of intimacy.

Both Allison and Bart started to visit me. They were motivated to make changes by their *shared pain*. In Bart's mental shed, the image of the lonely one had been tucked away in a corner too. Allison and Bart simply had devised different ways to deal with the pictured experience. The emotional struggle led to change—they stepped into their pictures. But there would have been no awareness without the pain. Knowing discontent for what it is, in some measure, is to escape its tyranny. As pain jolts knowledge loose, the ensuing tension excites a deeper reality. There are some things you can only learn through discontent, which cannot be learned in a safe place, in "Brooklyn." Perhaps the reason behind the failure of children of famous people is that they are always living in the light. They are never exposed to the darkness where both seeds and persons grow.

The third learning condition fills the pages of the Bible. The wilderness, weighted with emotional pressure, is a common educational setting. It was for Abraham, Elijah, John the Baptist, and Jesus. In the wasteland the lights are out; the supports are gone; the telephones are silent. No arrows. No street signs. The old, comfortable mental pictures begin to blur. At first you are confused, then agitated, grieved, ·or numbed. But you come to a turning point. Either you will resist the pain of self-reflection or you will be drawn into it. If drawn, certain questions recur. What has life done with you? What have you failed to do with life? What is your own responsibility for the disappointment you experience? What strengths have you overlooked and not exercised to deal with your circumstances? What practical changes do you have the capacity to make? What changes are outside your capacity?

Experiences of near despair are referred to as "cleansings." Room must be made in your mental shed for new pictures. You cannot escape reality and its challenge to your mind-set. You cannot delegate your contentment to something or someone outside yourself. Nor can you delegate your discontent to something or someone else, scapegoating others and claiming innocence. You cannot remedy the discontent, moreover, by continually living underneath your feelings. In the wilderness neither blood nor alliances, neither objects nor answers, neither blamings nor demands bring you contentment. You are thrown upon yourself. What *responses* will you make?

A training ground

When thrown upon himself, the apostle Paul learned that discontent yields only when confronted day by day, step by step, thorn by thorn, with a consistent attack. Whatever the circumstances, contentment or discontent, what counted was the empowerment of Christ. So empowered, Paul knew that God's gracious purpose was taking place though appearances denied it, feelings opposed it, mental pictures did not confirm it. Faith is the imaginative power which pictures meanings yet to be revealed (hope), strength beyond the self and the moment (promise), God's working for the good (love), beginning again (forgiveness).

For Paul, contentment itself is never the goal of life. Contentment, as well as discontent, are only pictures in your head, only views of life based on your limited experiences. Thus contentment and discontent are not circumstances, things, or something outside yourself. As Paul mentions, *he* had to learn to be content. The change occurred *within* Paul. In any and all situations, Paul imagined that everything is possible with God; the rest was faith and courage.

Life is a training ground where again and again you step into your pictures. Hence Paul knew that you cannot walk by "sight," that is, the pictures which you form from your own experiences. Rather, you walk by "faith," the picture of God's love revealed in Jesus Christ, which no experience of your own could ever reveal to you—yet can touch and change every picture you have.

An exercise that can help you use in your life the ideas from this chapter is printed on page 127 in the exercises section.

Exercises

The World inside You (p. 12)

The mental shed

The exercise below helps you discover some of the pictures which are stored in your mental shed. An example is given to assist you in completing the exercise. You are asked to describe briefly five significant experiences. For each of the five experiences, complete the columns headlined, *picture, feeling,* and *action.* Include both negative and positive experiences.

Experience	Picture	Feeling	Action
Example: A German shepherd dog chases me up a tree at age five or six.	Fierce dog	Pain	Freeze body
(1)			
(2)			
(3)			
(4)			
(5)			

In this activity, as well as those which follow, if you are part of a group, share your responses.

Setting Yourself Up for Disappointment (p. 22)

Beliefs that cause disappointment

The statements below are beliefs that set you up for disappointment. They look at things from only one perspective. Circle the ones which are contained in your mental shed. What would you need to do to see more clearly?

I believe that:

1. Life should be fair.
2. Almost every problem has a perfect solution.
3. There is always one right way and one true love.
4. Happy people don't get angry.
5. Adults don't ask for help.
6. Good people don't criticize.
7. I am not as good as others.
8. I should be positive all the time.
9. I can't change my attitude.
10. My worries will go away if I don't think about them.
11. My problems would be solved if people helped me.
12. My problems have a magic cure.
13. People should act better.
14. People must be punished for their mistakes.
15. People ought to take care of me.
16. Crying is always childish.
17. Fighting is never helpful.
18. Doubting is not at all allowed.
19. Really, I do not have any problems.
20. What could you tell me that I don't already know?
21. Honestly, I'm happy every minute.
22. When luck rolls my way, I'll be satisfied.
23. When you change, I'll be in a better mood.
24. When all the facts are in hand, I'll make a decision.

Loosening the Grip of Wishful Thinking (p. 32)

Between wishful thinking and reality living

Circle a number (1-10) to rate yourself for each pair of statements below. Let *1* represent living in a state of wishful thinking and *10* living in reality. Where do you see yourself between the two poles?

Wishful Thinking   **Reality Living**

1. I wish I were   1 2 3 4 5 6 7 8 9 10   I am who I am.
2. Take care of me.   1 2 3 4 5 6 7 8 9 10   I will take care of myself and reach out to others.
3. If only . . .   1 2 3 4 5 6 7 8 9 10   Now that . . .
4. Finding the right person   1 2 3 4 5 6 7 8 9 10   Being the right person
5. Oh, I'm perfect!   1 2 3 4 5 6 7 8 9 10   Oh, I've got my faults, but there's good in me.
6. Contentment is your dreams coming true.   1 2 3 4 5 6 7 8 9 10   Contentment is a decision I make.
7. Good things happen to good people.   1 2 3 4 5 6 7 8 9 10   Good things happen.
8. Expect the possible.   1 2 3 4 5 6 7 8 9 10   Expect the possible but not all is probable.
9. There's a cure for everything.   1 2 3 4 5 6 7 8 9 10   Some things get resolved.
10. Make a wish!   1 2 3 4 5 6 7 8 9 10   Make a choice!
11. When the situation changes, I'll do better.   1 2 3 4 5 6 7 8 9 10   What you are doing is helping you.

Finding the Missing X (p. 42)

Expectation inventory

The left-hand column below is a list of needs. Are your expectations for the meeting of those needs too little, too much, something else, or realistic? Mark the appropriate column.

Needs	Too Little	Too Much	Something Else	Realistic
Survival and safety				
Touching and attention				
Guidance and counsel				
Participation and belonging				
Freedom and tolerance				
Acceptance and love				
Support and trust				
Accomplishment and mastery				
Enjoyment and play				
Nurturing and encouragement				
Purpose and meaning				
Faith and hope				

Glancing at your responses, what needs are part of your missing X? In what way do you need to adjust your expectations?

Taking a Psychological Bath (p. 54)

Out of the shadow

Carl Jung coined the term "the Shadow." It is a concept referring to the dark, unwanted side of your personality. These characteristics run contrary to the person you want to be. Thus they are rejected or hidden. The simplest way to deal with your Shadow is to deny its existence, but then you project your dark side onto other people. You think you are clean and bright while others are actually bearing your darkness.

In this exercise you are asked to examine the characteristics of your dark side, your Shadow; the very things you are most apt to reject in yourself and to project onto others.

(1) Make a list of 10 favorable characteristics or desirable traits which are part of your personality (what you want to be).

(2) Write the opposite of each characteristic. Example: Favorable Characteristic—Faith; Opposite Characteristic—Doubt. The list of 10 *opposites* contains elements of your Shadow, parts of yourself that you would disown and project.

(3) Who are the people you blame the most? What people are you usually shaming? Who are you asking to bear your own discontent?

Who Said Life Was Fair? (p. 64)

Beyond unfairness

Many things in life escape reason and explanations; they can only be outgrown. Using the diagram below, describe an unfair event or state of affairs in your life. Begin with the early experiences. Describe both what happened outside of yourself (circumstance) and what happened inside of yourself (attitude, feeling). Then proceed to a description of the mid-experiences, and finally summarize the growth that occurred in the advanced experiences. The following questions are given to help you get started.

What kind of *brooding* did you use?

How did you *banish* the event from awareness in order to overcome the unfairness?

What other *reactive* mechanisms were operative? Blame? Withdrawal? Anger? Pleasing?

How much *time* was involved?

What *resources* were most beneficial in dealing with the event?

How did you *grow?*

What new *attitudes* or *perceptions* do you now have to deal with your own incompleteness and life's limitations?

Advanced Experiences

Mid Experiences

Early Experiences

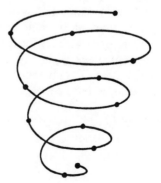

Contentment Is Yours (p. 73)

Rating your contentment

Rate each area of your life in the listing below, using a scale of 1 (discontented) to 10 (contented). Circle the appropriate number.

	Discontented					Contented				
Friends and social life	1	2	3	4	5	6	7	8	9	10
Work or primary activity	1	2	3	4	5	6	7	8	9	10
Being in love	1	2	3	4	5	6	7	8	9	10
Recognition, success	1	2	3	4	5	6	7	8	9	10
Sex life	1	2	3	4	5	6	7	8	9	10
Personal growth	1	2	3	4	5	6	7	8	9	10
Mental/emotional well-being	1	2	3	4	5	6	7	8	9	10
Physical health	1	2	3	4	5	6	7	8	9	10
Body and attractiveness	1	2	3	4	5	6	7	8	9	10
Finances, standard of living	1	2	3	4	5	6	7	8	9	10
Sense of purpose, life's meaning	1	2	3	4	5	6	7	8	9	10
The future, a living hope	1	2	3	4	5	6	7	8	9	10
Leisure, recreation	1	2	3	4	5	6	7	8	9	10
Time to do what you want	1	2	3	4	5	6	7	8	9	10
Religious convictions, feelings and activities	1	2	3	4	5	6	7	8	9	10

When you have finished your ratings, complete the following:

1. Add the 15 scores and average.   Average _____

2. Which item of discontent have you struggled with for the longest period of time?   Discontent Duration _____

3. Which item of contentment have you enjoyed for the longest period of time?   Contentment Duration _____

4. Which item(s) would you most want to change for greater contentment?   Item(s) for Change _____

_____

When Discontent Is a Blessing (p. 84)

Directions:

List below seven discontents you have experienced. Mark any statement in 1 and 2 that is appropriate to that experience. Total the number of checks in each column. Rank order A-J in column 1 and K-S in column 2. This exercise helps you understand how discontent has affected you and in what ways it has been a blessing.

1: When I experienced these things

A — I became confused, unsure of myself
B — I felt angry, hurt, and rejected
C — I blamed others
D — I felt alone, depressed; I withdrew
E — I brooded
F — I banished the suffering from my mind and heart
G — I changed some inner picture (belief, wish, or expectation)
H — I met a challenge or had an adventure
I — I sought help and support
J — I accepted what I couldn't change, and changed what I could, knowing the difference between the two

2: As a result of these experiences

K — I learned something new
L — I received acceptance and love
M — I felt what I did was important, significant
N — I changed my behavior
O — I became aware of things
P — I felt at ease, at one with myself
Q — I gave comfort to others
R — I gave proportion to the ideal and the real
S — I accepted my weakness

Seven Discontents	A	B	C	D	E	F	G	H	I	J	K	L	M	N	O	P	Q	R	S
(1)																			
(2)																			
(3)																			
(4)																			
(5)																			
(6)																			
(7)																			
TOTAL the check marks in each column																			
RANK ORDER the totals in each set of responses (1 and 2)																			

The Restless Heart (p. 96)

Between limits and longings

Longings:	Limits:
Whole	Incomplete
Related	Lonely
Knowledge	Blindness
Trust	Security
Hope	Despair
Peace	Hostility
Thankful	Resentful
Eternal Life	Death
Forgiveness	Sin
_____	_____

You live between limits and longings. Above, nine limits are matched with nine longings. Below is a list of questions, to help you discover where you experience the greatest pull and tug.

Which pair of opposites are most painful for you? (*There is space to write down one of your own choices on the bottom.*)
Where do you go for relief?

Which limits do you experience most?

Which longings most frequently are satisfied?

What spiritual resources strengthen you?

Stepping into the Picture (p. 107)

In any and all circumstances

Briefly below describe old pictures you held in your mental shed (A, B, C). Then in the lower row note how the old picture became a new picture of yourself (D, E, F). Answer the questions for each set of pictures (A-D, B-E, C-F).

(A) Old Picture   (B) Old Picture   (C) Old Picture

(D) New Picture   (E) New Picture   (F) New Picture

Questions:

	A	B	C

1. Was this picture based on your beliefs, wishes or expectations?
2. Did you blame, brood, or banish when disappointed?
3. What was the learning environment for your change of pictures— a safe place, a new experience, an emotional struggle?

	D	E	F

4. What was the blessing of your discontent?
5. Who was your guide?
6. What biblical image was beneficial?